MW01145541

IMAGES
of America

ST. ANDREWS

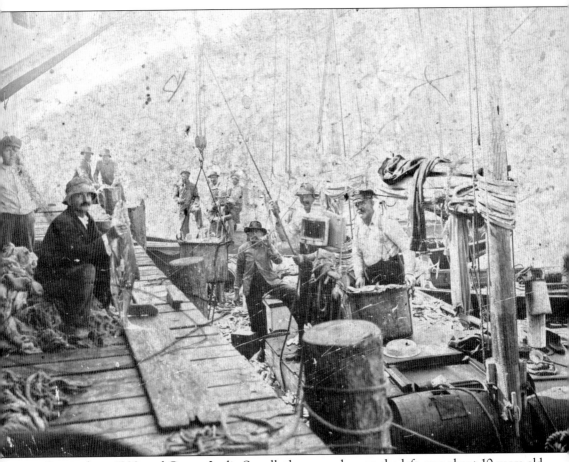

It was about 1900, and George Leslie Sowell, the young boy on the left, was about 10 years old when he participated in the fishing trip pictured. "Les" was the son of Jesse and Betty Sowell. Fishing—as an industry, as a sport, and as a resource for the family dinner table—has been central to the economy of the St. Andrews Bay area. Photographs of all aspects of fishing can be seen throughout this book. The photograph was loaned by James Sowell, who is George Leslie's son. (James Sowell [JS].)

ON THE COVER: "The *Lulu* is well-known to our people as a commodious and sea-worthy boat having formerly been owned by Mr. Tom Masker of St Andrews. Captain B. Pierce of Apalachicola who bought the *Lulu* is inaugurating a tri-weekly service between St Andrews and Apalachicola, leaving the city dock here on Tuesday, Thursday and Saturday, at 8 a.m., arriving at Apalachicola about 4 p.m. Westbound he will leave Apalachicola at 7:30 a.m. on Monday, Wednesday and Friday." The report in the May 13, 1915 *Panama City Pilot* continued to state that "Capt Pierce . . . was a Panama city visitor today, having come through the canal on his boat 'Lulu'. Capt Pierce was accompanied on his initial trip by Mr. Weeding of Apalachicola and several members of the baseball team from that city." (Herman Jones III [HJ].)

IMAGES
of America

ST. ANDREWS

Ann Pratt Houpt in association with
the St. Andrews Waterfront Partnership

ARCADIA
PUBLISHING

Copyright © 2007 by Ann Pratt Houpt in association with the St. Andrews Waterfront
Partnership
ISBN 978-0-7385-4426-7

Published by Arcadia Publishing
Charleston SC, Chicago IL, Portsmouth NH, San Francisco CA

Printed in the United States of America

Library of Congress Catalog Card Number: 2006939376

For all general information contact Arcadia Publishing at:
Telephone 843-853-2070
Fax 843-853-0044
E-mail sales@arcadiapublishing.com
For customer service and orders:
Toll-Free 1-888-313-2665

Visit us on the Internet at www.arcadiapublishing.com

This book is dedicated to the many people in the past, present, and future, pictured or not, who hold St. Andrews dear to their hearts and have been part of her history. The book also is dedicated to the next person to publish a St. Andrews book, in hopes you can use the many pictures that were beyond our allotted number!

CONTENTS

ACKNOWLEDGMENTS

Acknowledging everyone who contributed to this book is a task we will not undertake. Reading the book and looking at the pictures, readers may identify the donors by the key and the list of contributors. To all who brought pictures or called with historical information or names of people to contact, we give our thanks.

I would like to acknowledge the rich sources of local history provided by local authors, beginning with George M. West's *St. Andrews* of the early days of the community, Judge Ira Hutchison's *Some Who Passed This Way*, and Harold Bell's *Glimpses of the Panhandle*, as well as current authors Marlene Womack, Jeannie Cooper, Winston Chester, Richard Holley, and Glenda A. Walters. We are all presenting our own research and memories of a wealth of local history.

The book would not exist without the help of Rebecca Saunders, president of the Historical Society of Bay County and local history specialist at Bay County Public Library. Many thanks also to Mona Anita Lucas and Jeannie Cooper in the library's Local History Room for scanning the hundreds of photographs brought in by contributors.

KEY TO PHOTOGRAPH SOURCES

JLA: Judy and Louie Andrews
MAB: Margaret Arnold Boone
JDTB: JoDell Tiller Breland
RC: Robert Cain Sr.
HSAC: Historic St. Andrews Church
TLC: Trinity Lutheran Church
MAD: Margaret Anderson Duncan
MTD: Mary Tucker Dyer
DE: Dianne Eaton
SF: Surber family
SG: Shirley Gilmore
JG: Janet Givens
TRG: Teresa Rabon Goodwin
VSH: Victoria Stephens Helms
JH: John Hentz
HJ: Herman Jones III
BCPL: Bay County Public Library
    History Room
MJTL: Mrs. J. T. Locke
CJ: Christine Jamieson
JL: Janice Lucas
AGL: Anita Gleitsman Lucas
EDM: Ellen Day Maplesden
BM: Bobby Martin

JM: Jack Mashburn
RM: Ray Moates
PCM: Patsy C. Moates
CHM: Clifford H. Munson
AO: Ashley Olive
HP: Howard Padgett Jr.
ALP: Ann Lisenby Parmer
SAWP: St. Andres Waterfront Partnership
JDP: Jim and Doris Pigneri
HRR: Howard and Rosella Ridings
AJR: Albert J. Rowell
OTES: Oakland Terrace Elementary School
SLS: Sheila Leto Scott
DTS: Dr. Tim Smith
JS: James Sowell
KS: Kathy Swigler
BT: Bill Tant
TSV: Terry Scott Vickmark
BW: Buddy West
GMW: George Mortimer West Collection
LWHW: Lenora Windham Holman Warriner
BMO: Beatrice Moates
JFS: Jerry F. Sowell

INTRODUCTION

St. Andrews has been an excellent place to live for as long as people have inhabited the Americas. During the last Ice Age, with sea levels as much as 350 feet lower than the present, a pathway was forged from this area all the way to Alaska that then traversed an exposed land bridge between northwest North America and Asia. Pleistocene animals easily traveled across this land bridge, and they were eventually pursued by hunter-gatherers in search of game. The fossil remains of mammoth, mastodon, saber-toothed cat, and camel have been found in the upland spring runs and creeks that feed St. Andrews Bay.

Locally found artifacts attest to the fact that Native Americans have been in our area for at least 13,000 years. When people first arrived here, the sea level was still nearly 100 feet below present levels, and the Gulf shoreline was about 15 miles farther south. Our bay was mostly high and dry with Econfina Creek creating a valley running towards the Gulf. This means that the coastal forests and embayments that they encountered are now submerged offshore and the then interior river valleys flooded to create today's area deepwater bays, such as St. Andrews Bay.

Local Native Americans had a rich and varied culture that changed through time in response to changes in climate conditions, resource availability, technological improvements, and population increases. As the Ice Age waned, less hunting gave way to more gathering, as can be evidenced by the numerous shell middens scattered along St. Andrews Bay (an ancient midden and occupation site is located within Oaks by the Bay Park). From 5,000 to about 2,500 years ago, some of these middens evolved into mounds for interment of the dead. By 700 A.D., these mounds had temples constructed upon them, and there had developed a vigorous trade of locally crafted shell goods that found their way to places as distant as Minnesota and New York.

At contact with the Spanish around 1500, the area was inhabited by the Chatot and Yucci tribes. Shortly after contact, the Chatot became extinct (as did over 90 percent of Florida native peoples) and the Yucci escaped such a fate by dispersing to the north and west. The area gradually became peopled again around 1700 A.D. and later on by Creeks and Cherokees who had evaded the relocation to the West that culminated in the Trail of Tears in the 1830s. By this time, many white settlers had moved into the area and the Native American tribal group known as the Seminoles moved into south Central Florida and the Everglades.

The first European settlement in the St. Andrews Bay area was along Beach Drive between Frankford Avenue and Lake Caroline. Retired Georgia governor John Clark and his wife, Nancy, built a home and lived there from 1827 until their deaths in 1832. Just a few people resided year-round in St. Andrews, earning a living making salt, fishing, and boarding vacationers who came to the area for the "healthy sea baths" and the fishing.

By the mid-1800s, the summer population was 1,200–1,500. The Clark home was converted to a hotel known as the Tavern. One visitor to the hotel was noted Southern writer Caroline Hentz. Lake Caroline was named for her. In 1845, the town was referred to as St. Andrews by the post office. The geodetic survey of 1855, the first official survey, showed the town as St. Andrews City and the bay was called St. Andrews Bay. In 1902, the post office accidentally left the "s" off and never corrected it. The *St. Andrews Bay News*, printed by George M. West in the early 1900s, listed the town as St. Andrews but referred to the post office as St. Andrew. Most continue to refer to the town as St. Andrews.

During the Civil War, the town was a strategic supplier of salt to the Confederate troops, which made it a target for the North. Many raids were made in the area by Federal troops, and eventually the town was destroyed in 1863.

Lambert Ware visited the area in 1877 and then returned in 1879. His brother Francis joined him in 1882, and they operated Ware Mercantile and Ware's Wharf on the present Harbour Village and St. Andrews Marina sites, respectively. The town flourished again with salt, fishing, boat building, and shipping along the Gulf Coast. About this time, the St. Andrews Bay Railroad, Land, and Mining Company, locally known as the Cincinnati Company because they were based in that Ohio town, advertised mail-order real estate with this description:

> The loveliest location in all Florida. In a land where the genial climate of a winterless round of years will reward your every effort with the most bountiful harvests; where the summers are joyous seasons of refreshing breezes and invigorating nights of cool and healthful slumber; and where the winters are but bewitching contrasts to the summers in heightening and intensifying the delicious pleasure of a life in the fairest land the sun ever blessed with it's genial kiss. There is but one Florida, and St. Andrews Bay is its brightest jewel.

In the beginning, lots approximately 25 by 82 feet were sold for $1.25; later the price escalated to $8 for a lot in "St. Andrews by the sea." The scheme finally busted but not before some of the buyers decided they really liked the area and stayed.

In 1908, St. Andrews incorporated for the first time. It continued to grow in the early 1900s and became a popular port on the coast. The *Tarpon* traveled between Mobile and Apalachicola, stopping like clockwork in St. Andrews, delivering beer, flour, and other supplies. One could set one's watch by the arrival and departure of the *Tarpon*, and it was this persistence of her captain, and the fact she was overloaded, that led to her demise. He pushed her on through a storm to be on time, but she sank off Panama City Beach in 1937. The site is now an underwater archaeological preserve.

Other towns had grown up in the area, one of those being Panama City, which annexed St. Andrews and three other small towns in 1927.

Panama City became an important port and was used for building ships (and later dismantling them) during World War II. Clark Gable was here during that time and patronized local restaurants in St. Andrews. Charter boats, restaurants, and shops in St. Andrews were bustling with people in the mid-1900s. The community was a destination. The center of attention shifted as Panama City Beach opened up to traffic. In the 1980s, commerce in St. Andrews took a sharp dive as the business community left for the "new" territory in Panama City Beach.

The Panama City Commission recognized the need to revitalize St. Andrews and the potential there. In 1989, St. Andrews was designated as a Community Redevelopment Area. That, and a variety of grants from the State of Florida in the form of cash and technical assistance, has been used as the tools for revitalizing St. Andrews into a sustainable waterfront community. The redevelopment process has been an innovative, successful partnership between the city and the citizens.

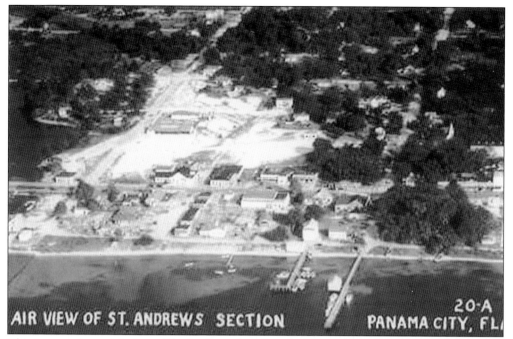

This is an early, aerial view of St. Andrews found in the library's Local History Room. No date was given. (BCPL.)

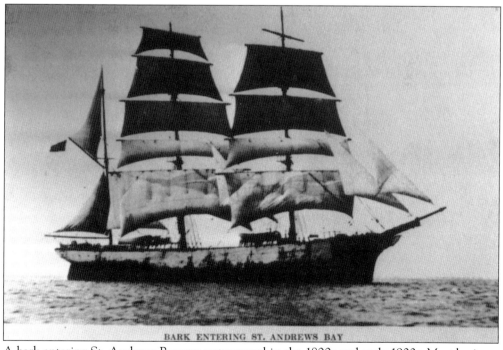

A bark entering St. Andrews Bay was not unusual in the 1800s and early 1900s. Most business was conducted by ship. The bay provided a large deepwater harbor for ships. Away from the shore, roads were almost nonexistent. (BCPL.)

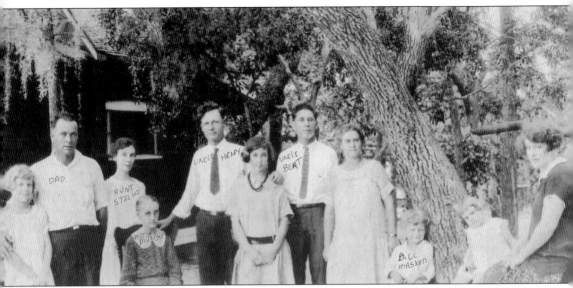

This photograph of a family gathering on Lake Huntington probably was taken by Ed Masker (since he is not in the picture). Shown from left to right are his daughter, Phoebe Masker (Fowhand); Bill Munson; Jestella Munson Masker; Mrs. ? Munson; Henry Munson; unidentified; Bert Munson; unidentified; Bill Masker (son of Ed Masker); unidentified; and Minnie Munson. They are in front of Ed Masker's home on Cincinnatti Avenue at Huntington Bayou. Thanks to Masker's photography and the postcards he produced, there is a good account of family history of the area. (CHM.)

One

OLD TOWN

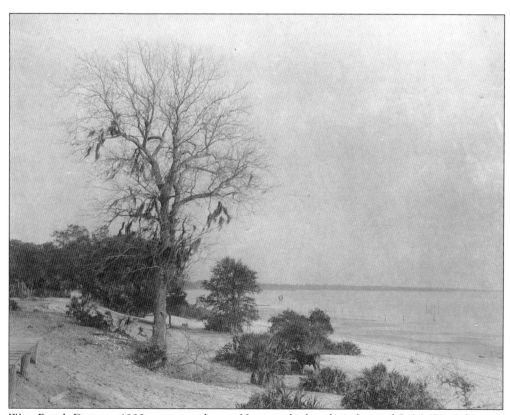

West Beach Drive in 1890 was just a dream. Here on the beach in front of G. M. West's lots, we see a hickory tree and a path that went from house to house along the beach. To the left of the cow is where the road (Beach Drive) would be built. (GMW.)

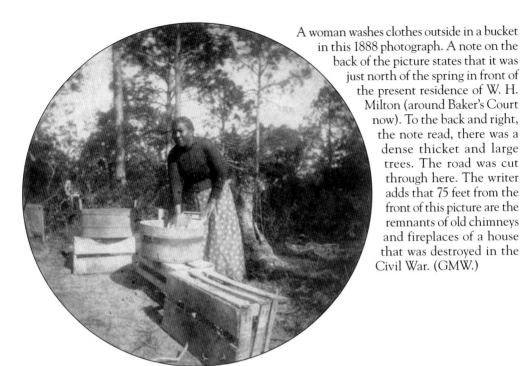

A woman washes clothes outside in a bucket in this 1888 photograph. A note on the back of the picture states that it was just north of the spring in front of the present residence of W. H. Milton (around Baker's Court now). To the back and right, the note read, there was a dense thicket and large trees. The road was cut through here. The writer adds that 75 feet from the front of this picture are the remnants of old chimneys and fireplaces of a house that was destroyed in the Civil War. (GMW.)

In this December 1887 photograph, a woman is sitting under a tree by the side of the lane. George Mortimer West wrote on the back of the photograph: "This shows the front of the lot now owned by Mrs Milton and a road that was used by me in getting material from Ware's Wharf which was brought through woods and along the beach until Spring Run was crossed and then northeasterly to a gate I had in my west fence. On the lower right is shown Jones thicket that was in front of the oaks where Witherill brothers had their boat yard." (GMW.)

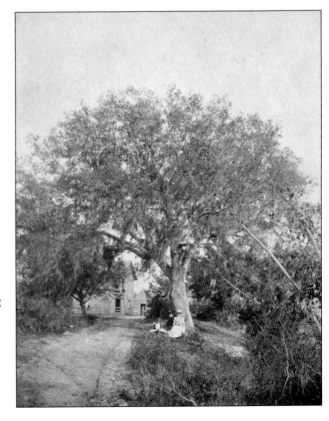

Two men and two women are removing fish from a seine net on the bay beach. The people are unidentified. From early settlement to modern times, private and commercial fishermen used nets to catch mullet and other fish. This important industry continued to be a major contribution to the area economy until the state declared a ban on seine nets in November 1994. (GMW.)

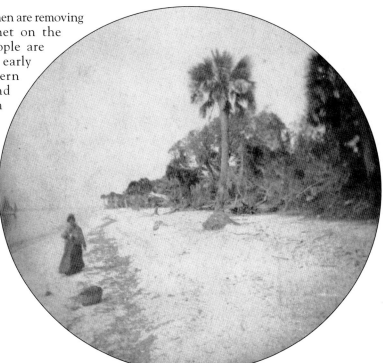

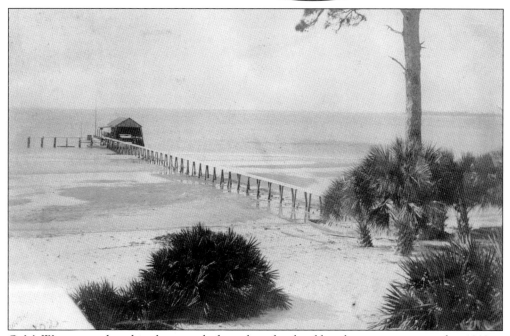

G. M. West states that this photograph shows his wharf and boathouse as it appeared in 1902 or 1903: "A new wharf was just built over this one. I had a wing on the wharf then as shown. The boat which I bought in 1902 is shown alongside the wharf. At that time I put seats under the palms, not shown in the picture, and seats on the parkway in front of my lots on cedar trees. I used the beach front as part of my place and had it ornamented in various ways." (GMW.)

13

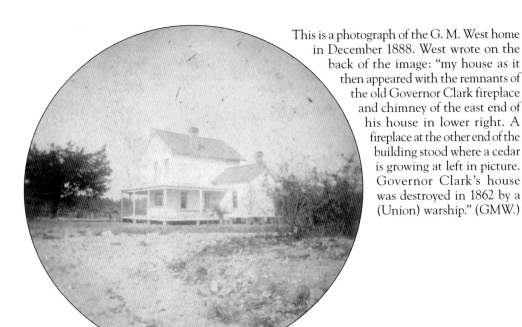

This is a photograph of the G. M. West home in December 1888. West wrote on the back of the image: "my house as it then appeared with the remnants of the old Governor Clark fireplace and chimney of the east end of his house in lower right. A fireplace at the other end of the building stood where a cedar is growing at left in picture. Governor Clark's house was destroyed in 1862 by a (Union) warship." (GMW.)

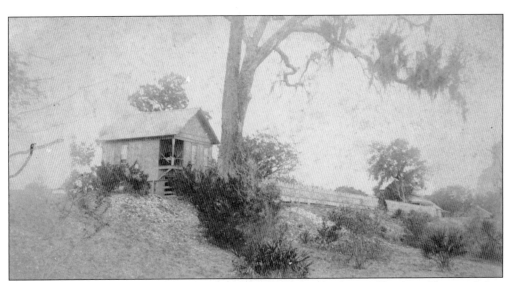

Taken in December 1888 by West, this photograph shows the front of his lots. He noted that this is where it was claimed the old road ran. This much later would become Beach Drive, which runs from the Cove to St. Andrews in Panama City. (GMW.)

George Mortimer West (here in 1880) was a writer, promoter, economist, horticulturist, publisher, and entrepreneur and was credited as the founding father of Panama City. Through his Gulf Coast Development Company, he drew national attention to St. Andrews and Panama City (known as "Harrison" at the time). West dreamed of a seaport in Panama City, Florida, with a railroad north to Chicago, linking Chicago with the Panama Canal and world trade. (BCPL.)

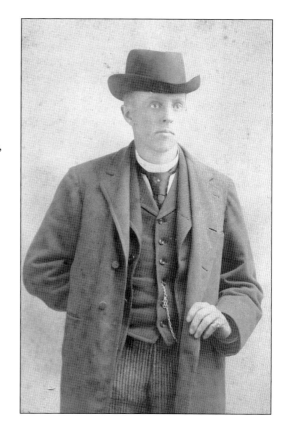

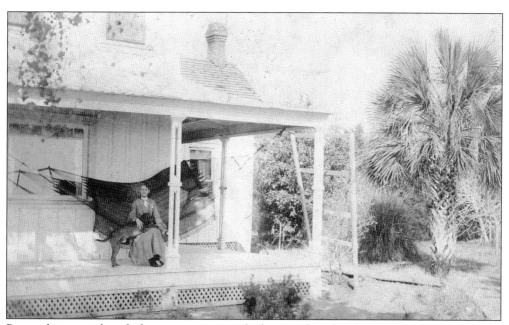

Pictured is an unidentified woman sitting on the hammock with a dog on the front porch of the West home c. 1900. (GMW.)

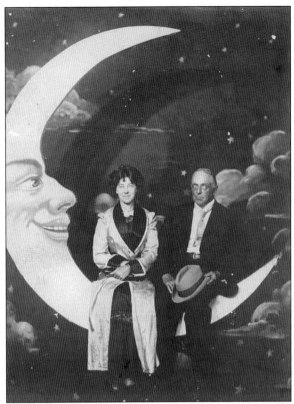

George Mortimer West sits in a half moon with who might be Lillian Carlisle West. Twice widowed, West, editor of the *Panama City Pilot* newspaper, married Lillian H. Carlisle of Callaway, Florida, in 1909. Lillian went on to serve as editor of the *St. Andrews Bay News*, the *Lynn Haven Free Press*, and the *Panama City Pilot* after Mr. West's death in 1926. (GMW.)

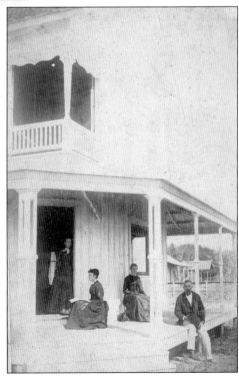

An unidentified group of people relaxes on the porch of the G. M. West home in this 1900 photograph. (GMW.)

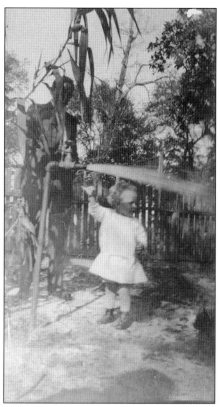
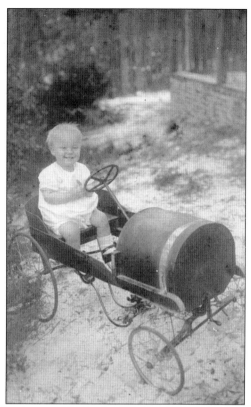

G. M. West's grandsons are shown in the yard of his home. Charles West (above left) plays with a spigot with a man in the background and (above right) poses in a kiddie car. In photograph below, Philip West's sons, Bay (left) and Charles, play with a goat and cart. (GMW.)

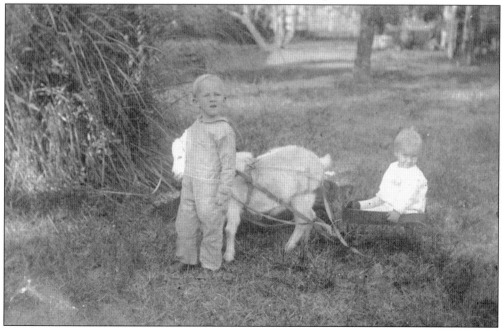

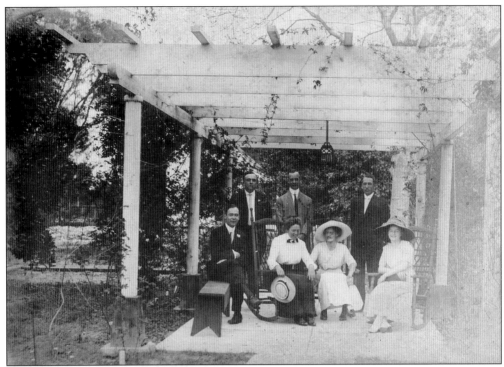

The porch in the backyard of the West home is the scene of this photograph dated sometime after 1909. Lillian C. West is second from left. Grace Wilson is third from left. The others are unidentified. (GMW.)

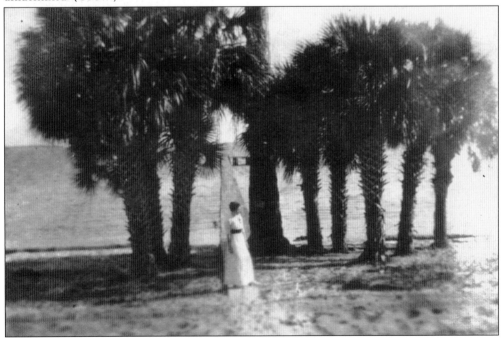

A young woman is pictured on the waterfront of the West home in 1912 with the wharf in the background. (GMW.)

Lillian Carlisle West is shown in a 1932 snapshot. On the back of the photograph it says, "Lillian's hair is snow white. She wears it short and curled and it is beautiful. She doesn't know I'm sending this to you. Mary E. Jones." (BW.)

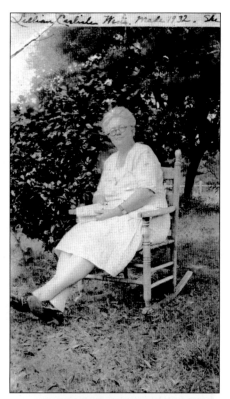

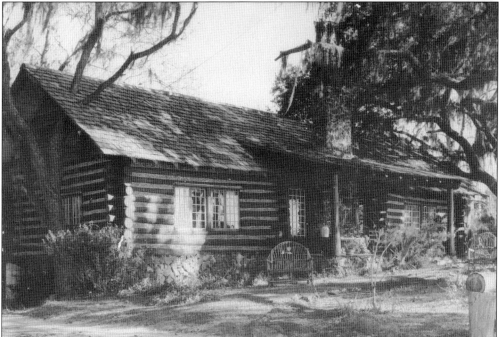

Lillian C. West built this log house adjacent to the original West home in 1934 on West Beach Drive in the Old Town neighborhood of St. Andrews. Her grandson Buddy West and his wife, Sylvia, reside here in 2007. (BW.)

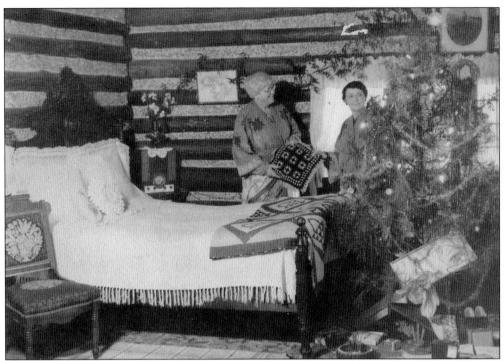

Lillian West, left, and her cousin Mary Jones are shown in the bedroom of the log house at Christmastime. (BW.)

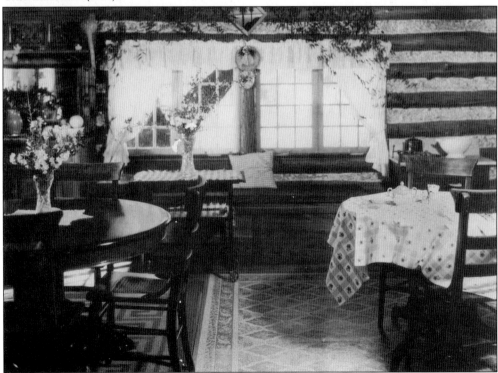

This photograph was taken in the dining room. Note there are two dining tables. (BW.)

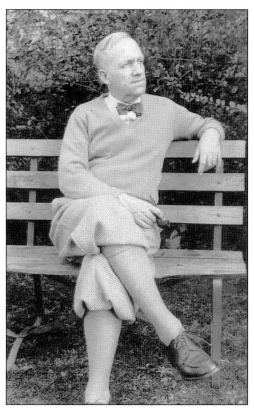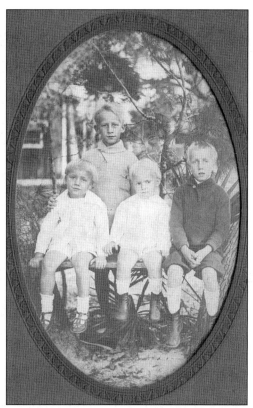

Phillip West is shown in the photograph at left. The right photograph is a portrait of Phillip and Maggie West's four sons, from left to right, Marion ("Bay"), George, Phillip, and Charles. (BW.)

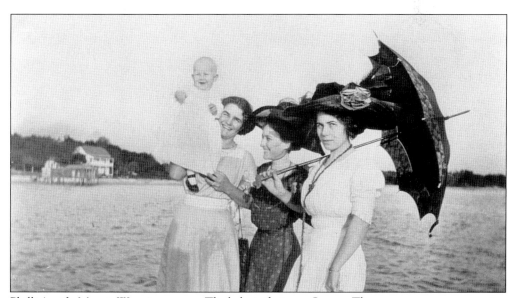

Phillip's wife, Maggie West, is at center. The baby is their son George. The two women accompanying her are unidentified. (BW.)

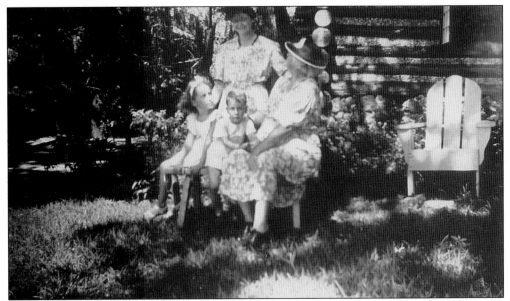

In the yard with their Aunt Mary and great-great-grandma Lillian West (right) are Betty (Haven) and Charles "Buddy" West. Buddy West operated the printing company after his great-great-grandmother's death until the City of Panama City purchased the building in October 2005. (BW)

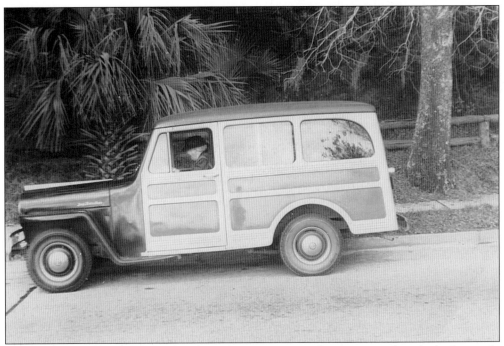

Lillian Carlisle West is seen driving her Willys van in St. Andrews. Once, when she had a wreck, the other driver and she both claimed fault. The other driver said, "I saw you coming from 3 blocks away and had ample time to turn off." (BW.)

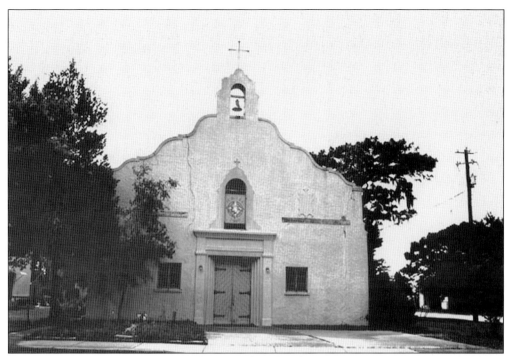

Construction of St. John the Evangelist Catholic Church, at 1008 Fortune Avenue, was started in April 1944. The church opened its doors for services on Christmas Eve, 1945. Adjacent to the church is the St. John's Catholic School. (HP.)

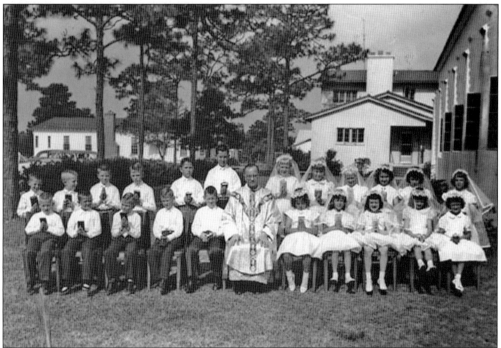

Shown here is a communion class with Fr. Leonard Pruzinski on the church grounds at St. John the Evangelist Catholic Church. (HP.)

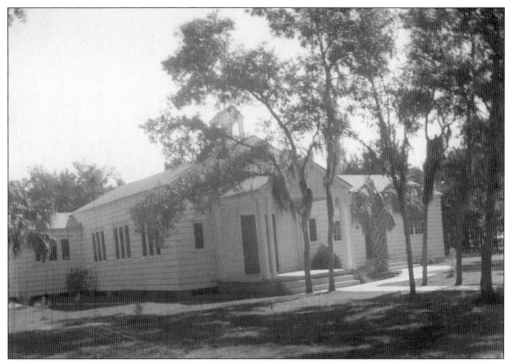

The old St. Andrews Episcopal Church building, originally situated on Beach Drive overlooking the bay, was relocated to Baldwin Road in 1940. (SLS.)

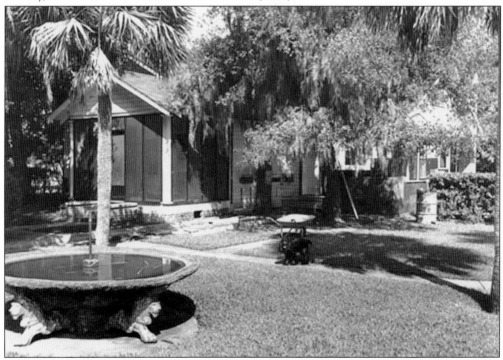

Newell and Ann Arnold owned this house at 2032 West Tenth Street. The property was sold to St. Andrews Methodist Church. The watering trough out front remians. (MAB.)

Two

LAKE CAROLINE

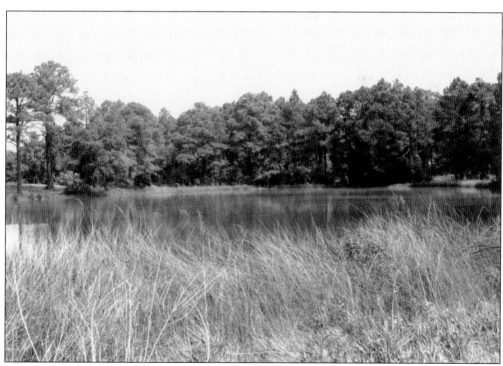

Flanked by East Caroline and West Caroline Boulevards, this lake is the center of the Lake Caroline neighborhood of St. Andrews. The area was a tourist destination in the mid-1800s, when families came from Marianna and other inland communities to enjoy the bay shores. Now it is a prosperous residential section of Panama City. (BCPL.)

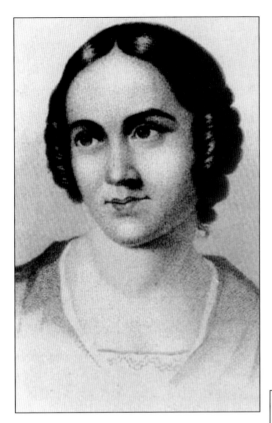

Caroline Lee Whiting Hentz, a noted author, spent time on St. Andrews Bay prior to the War between the States. Lake Caroline was named in her honor. From 1850 to 1856, she published eight novels and six collections of short stories. She died in Marianna, Florida, in 1856 of pneumonia. Her children published several more of her short-story collections after her death. Some of her novels are in the History Room of the Bay County Public Library. (BCPL.)

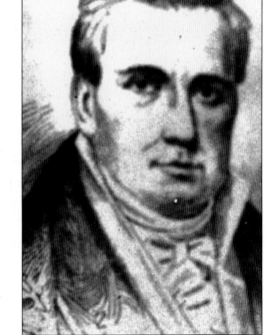

John Clark, a former governor of Georgia, moved to St. Andrews Bay with his family and built a log home near the intersection of Beach Drive and Frankford Avenue. He died in 1832. (BCPL.)

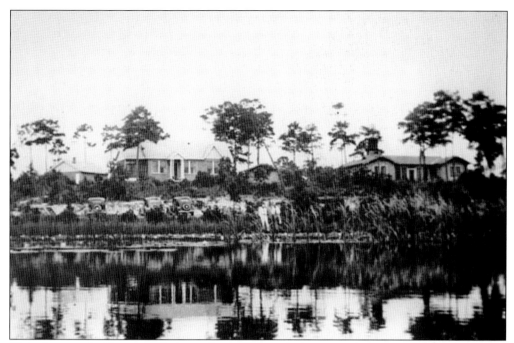

This photograph taken *c.* 1938 shows the A. H. Lisenby home on the west side of Lake Caroline near Eleventh Street. Dr. Lisenby established Lisenby Hospital on Eleventh Street in the Lake Caroline neighborhood. (ALP.)

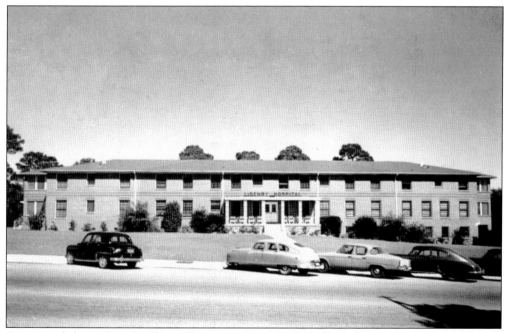

A postcard shows Lisenby Hospital *c.* 1940 at 1400 West Eleventh Street. The hospital later became Lisenby Retirement Center. (BCPL.)

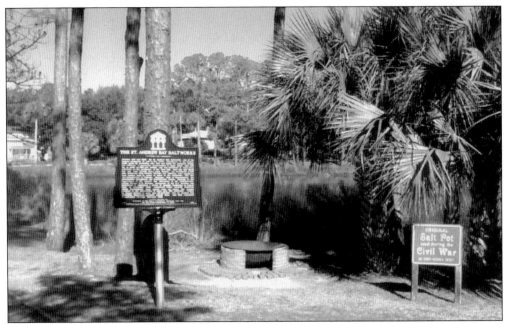

James Asbell Park is located on Lake Caroline at Beach Drive and East Caroline Boulevard. In 2000, when this photograph was taken, the Confederate Salt Kettle was located in this park. It is a favorite lunch spot for many downtown workers. (BCPL.)

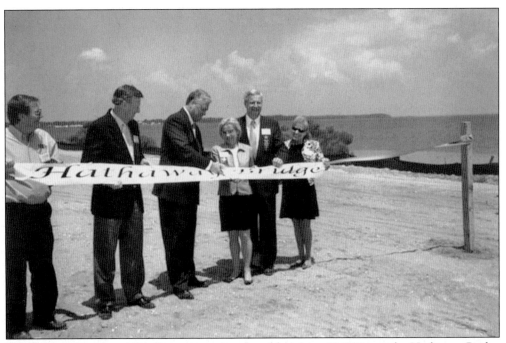

Florida House speaker Allen Bense is cutting the ribbon May 10, 2004, at the Hathaway Bridge dedication celebration. Elected to the Florida House of Representatives in 1998 and subsequently reelected, Bense served as Speaker of the House from 2004 to 2006. He and his wife and family reside in the Lake Caroline Neighborhood of St. Andrews on West Beach Drive. (BCPL.)

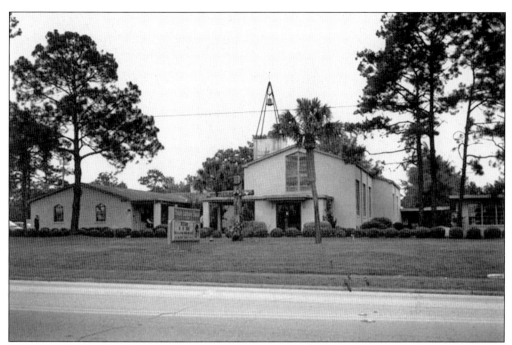

Trinity Lutheran Church was organized in 1952 and conducted worship services at the old city hall until the sanctuary was built and dedicated in 1954. This photograph in 1997 shows new additions to the social hall and the sanctuary. (TLC.)

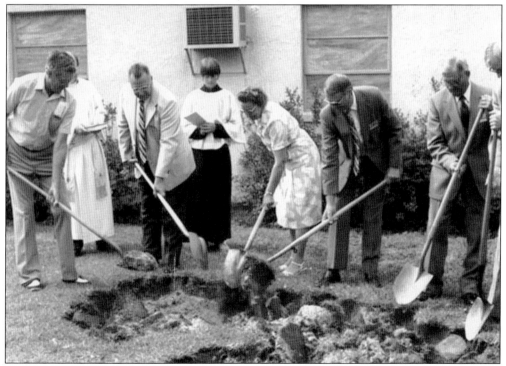

Members of Trinity Lutheran Church hold a groundbreaking ceremony for new additions to the social hall and sanctuary. (TLC.)

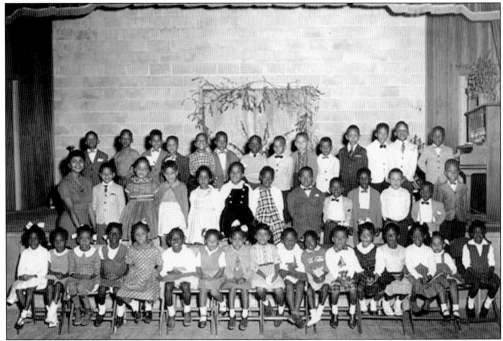

Trinity Lutheran Church erected an education building in which it held kindergarten for children of all races and denominations from 1956 until 1971, when the public school system initiated a kindergarten program. (TLC.)

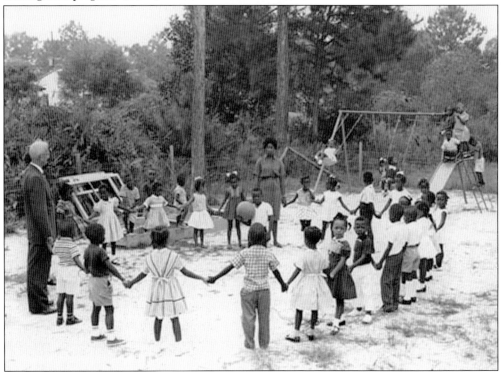

Shown here is a kindergarten class on the playground at Trinity Lutheran Church. (TLC.)

Kindergartners enjoy lunch with their classmates at Trinity Lutheran Kindergarten. (TLC.)

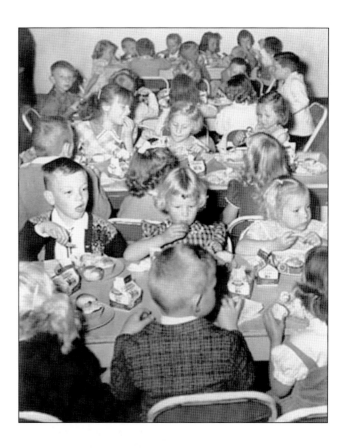

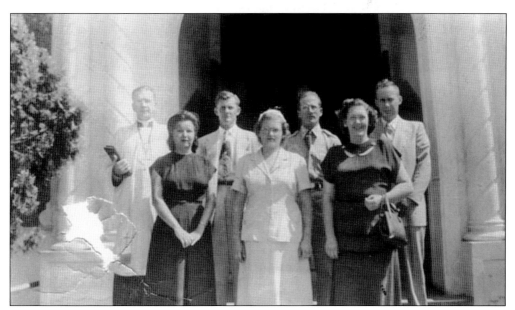

The first adult class of Trinity Lutheran Church is shown here on May 30, 1952, with the pastor, the Reverend Eduard Schack, who served from April 1952 to September 1954. (TLC.)

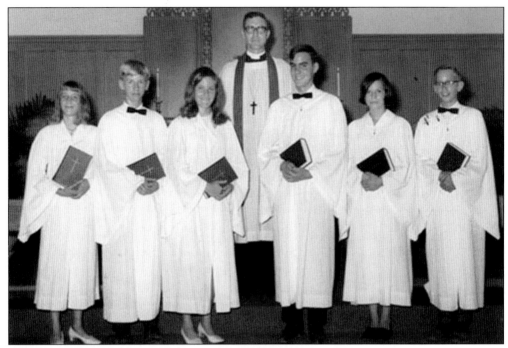

The Trinity Lutheran Church graduating class is pictured June 3, 1968. Pictured from left to right are Peggy Niesen, Kenneth Burke, Connie Niesen, Paul Cartia Jr., Patricia Barlow, and Curtis Trexler, with the Reverend Theodore Strelow, pastor from May 1965 to December 1969. (TLC.)

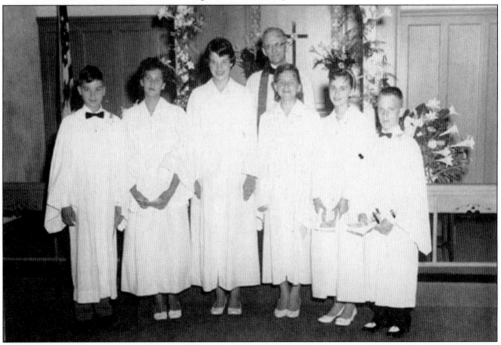

This undated picture of a graduating class at Trinity Lutheran Church includes, from left to right, Stephen Cooney, Mary Lou Lindholm, Marie Marsh, Karon Wilson, Brigitte Loine, and Ronald Jones. The pastor is unidentified. (TLC.)

Three

CINCINNATI HILL

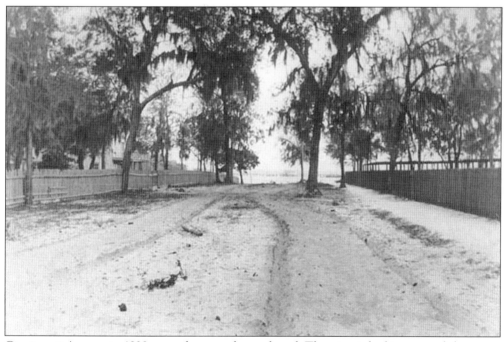

Cincinnati Avenue in 1898 was a deep, sand rutted road. The view is looking toward the water, and in the background on St. Andrews Bay, Ware's Wharf can be seen. (HJ.)

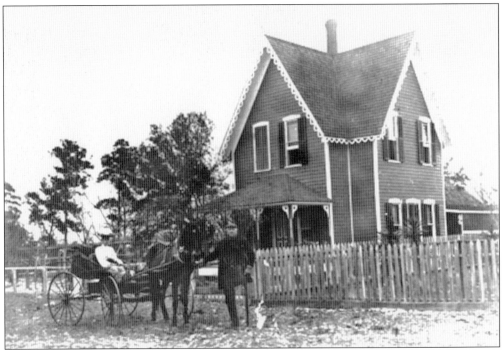

This house at 1406 Deer Avenue was built in 1887. Deer Avenue is just as sandy as Cincinnati but seems to have some grass growing in it. (BCPL.)

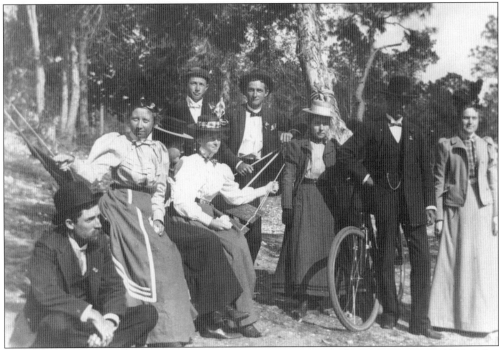

These friends are gathered for a photograph while enjoying outdoor recreation in 1890. John Gwaltney is seated at left. Merta Maxon is seated on the hammock next to him. The girls are all members of the Reading Girls Club. (HJ.)

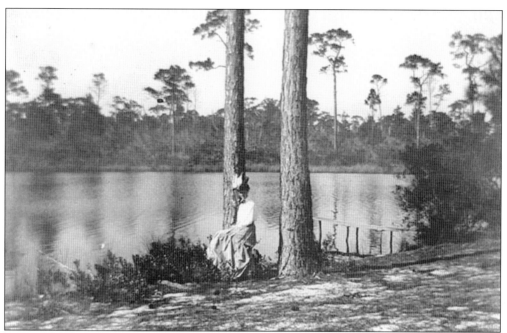

Zadie Ware (Mrs. Lambert Ware) is at the center of this tranquil scene by Lake Huntingdon in the Cincinnati Hill neighborhood c. 1900. (HJ.)

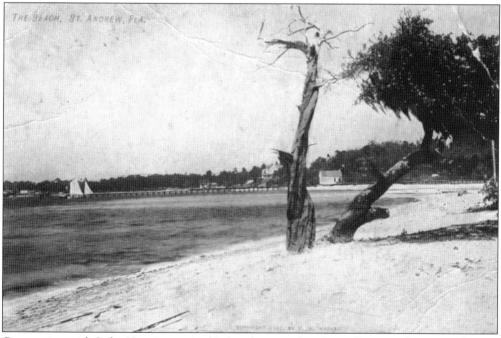

Contrasting with Lake Huntington is this beach scene showing sailboats and a pier with trees on shore long before development of the area. (JM.)

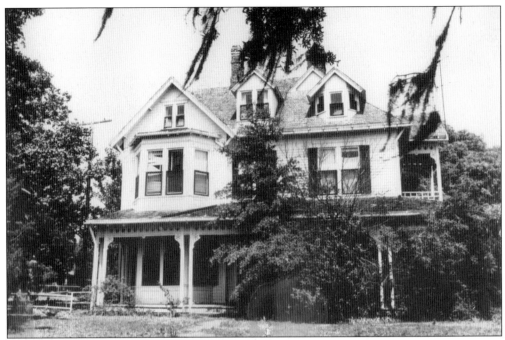

This house known as "The Villa" was a landmark in St. Andrews. On the back of the photograph is written "For Tim and Mary Ann Smith, St. Andrews 1856. Stephen and Annabelle Smith parents of Dr. Tim Smith." (DTS.)

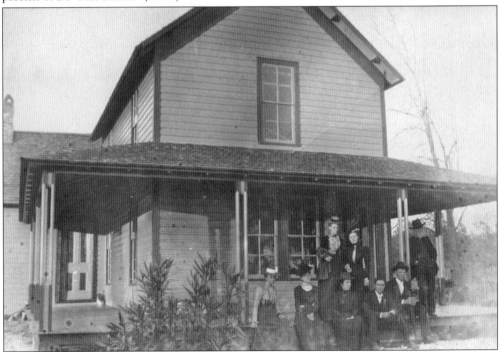

Family members gathered on the porch of the Gwaltney home include Mr. Gwaltney Sr., standing far right, and John Gwaltney, seated right, holding an umbrella. Others in the group are unidentified. (HJ.)

Stella Masker and Phoebe Masker (Fowhand) pose in a boat on Lake Huntington *c.* 1915. The house in the background was at the north end of Cincinnati Avenue. (CHM.)

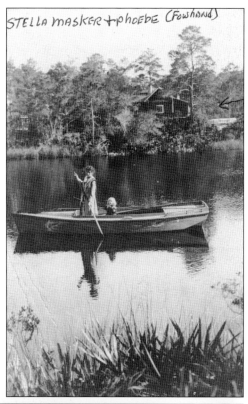

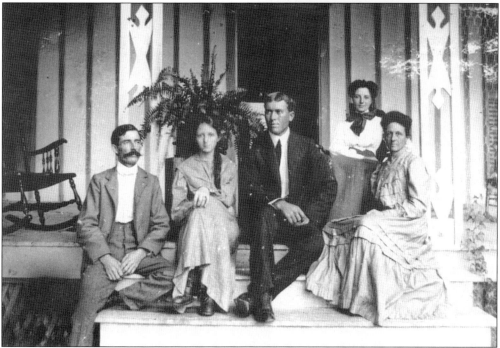

The Rose family is pictured on the porch of their home in 1900. Individuals are not identified by name. (BCPL.)

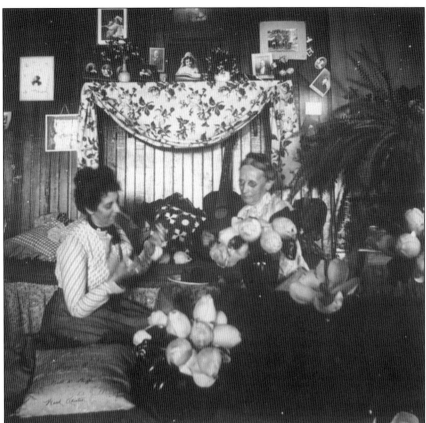

Mrs. Maxon, right, visits with her neighbor, Miss Rowland, in the Maxon home *c.* 1890. (HJ.)

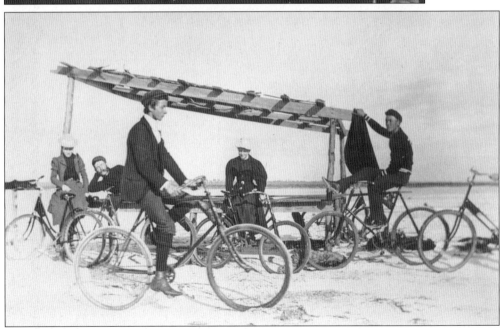

Merta Maxon is one of the girls in this group bicycling on the beach *c.* 1890. Visitors often came by train to Panama City and then by ferry to the beach. (HJ.)

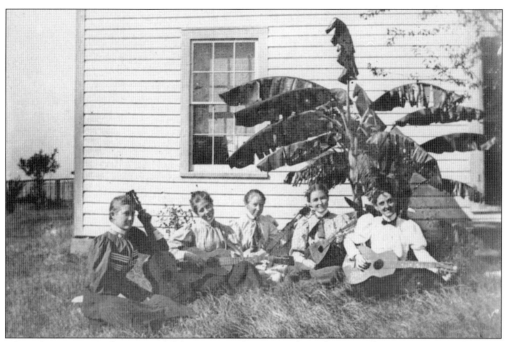

Merta Maxon is at the center of this group of young girls with musical instruments in the yard of the Maxon home on Lake Avenue *c.* 1898. (HJ.)

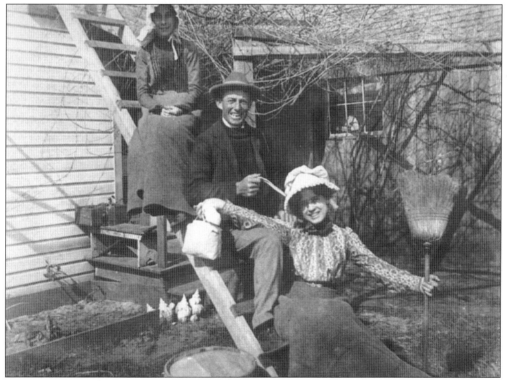

A young man and two young women pose on a ladder in the backyard *c.* 1890. Note the conch shells under the ladder. (HJ.)

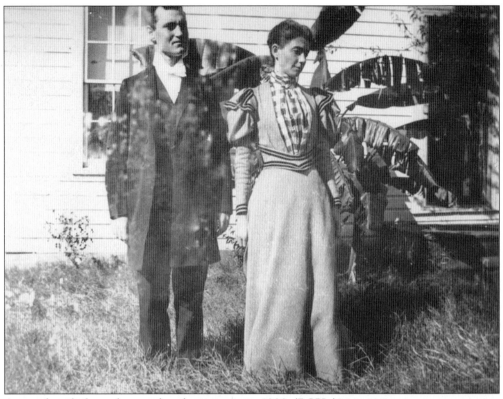

An unidentified couple poses by a banana tree *c.* 1900. (BCPL.)

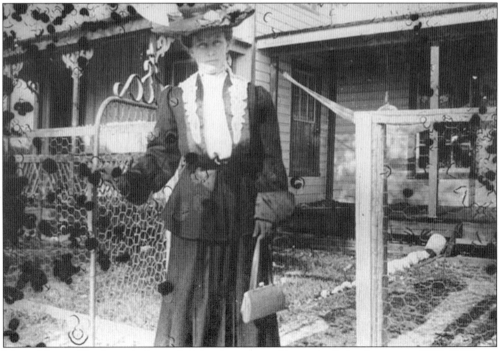

Merta Maxon Gwaltney is shown leaving her parents' home on Lake Avenue *c.* 1900. (HJ.)

This is the St. Andrews Presbyterian Church as it looked *c.* 1936. The church was organized September 13, 1886, and met in several homes. The first pastor was the Reverend E. H. Post, grandfather of Richard Post, a longtime teacher at Jinks Junior High School. The members raised money and helped construct a building, which was ready on July 22, 1888. (BCPL.)

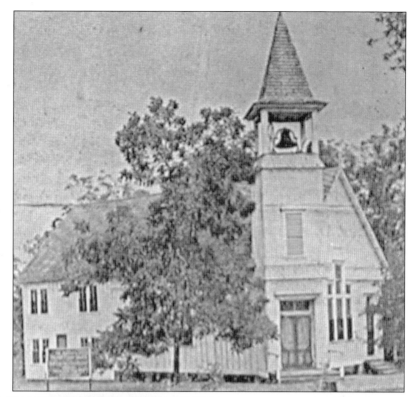

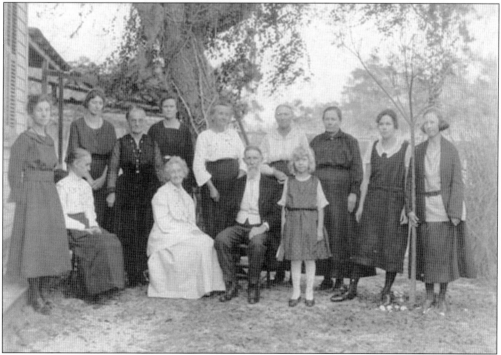

Neta Surber is standing center in this photograph of the Women's Auxiliary of St. Andrews Presbyterian Church. Nell Surber Ware is standing at the far right. (SF.)

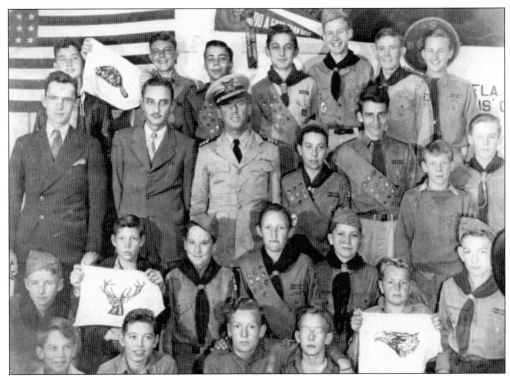

Boy Scout Troop 38 met at the St. Andrews Presbyterian Church. Present at this meeting in 1942 were, from left to right, (first row) Herbert Cowan, Gordon Youngblood, Tony Youngblood, and Hoke Grant Jr.; (second row) Randolph Cross, Fred Moates, James Thomas, Edwin Harmon, Bill Rowell, Bud Arnold, and John Lowther; (third row) Howard Sapp, James Warren, Tom Bingham, E. P. Cherry, James Kent, Jack Laird, and Tommy Thompson; (fourth row) Edwin Brogdon, Miller Lowther, John Lattner, Ernest Tweedle, Wallace Laird Jr., Lee Cowan, and Richard Post. (AJR.)

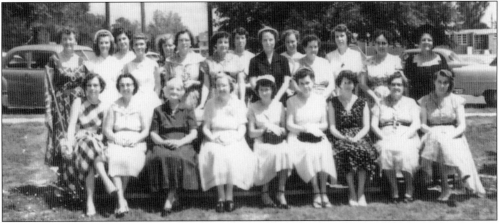

The women's Sunday school class taught by Carrie Daugherty met outside the St. Andrews Presbyterian Church for this photograph in 1958. From left to right are, (first row) Inis Surber, Orene Retherford, Roberta Daffin, Carrie Daugherty, Margarite Hollis, Barbara Hidle, unidentified, Marie Hill, and Kate Hayes; (second row) Lucille Wasson, Alice Scott, unidentified, Shirley Jones, unidentified, Marie Liese, Helen Holley, Edna Kelley, Eula Brown, Doris Arnold, Sue Maloy, Mrs. ? Davenport, Grace Muterspaugh, and Maud Arnold. (BCPL.)

Mary Hiller, teacher, and her Sunday school class from St. Andrews Presbyterian Church gathered outdoors for a photograph. They include Doug Hoskins, Matt Ellis, Julie Cook, Ruth Webb, David Jowers, Mitch Holman, Paul O'Rourke, Leslie Hay, Doc Rich, David Post, Angela Baggett, Pam Broussard, Gene Taylor, Renee Scott, and Buddy Arnold. (LWHW.)

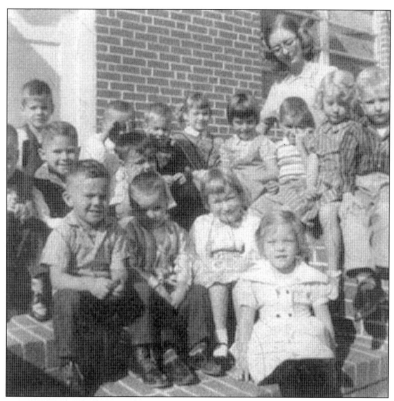

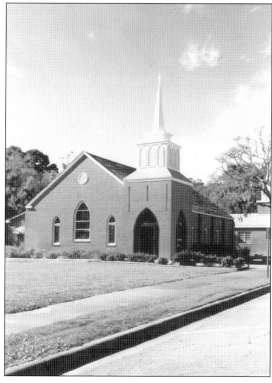

This is the St. Andrews Presbyterian Church in 2004 on the corner of Beck Avenue and Fourteenth Street. The Reverend Joe Vaughn came in 2002 and is currently pastor. (BCPL.)

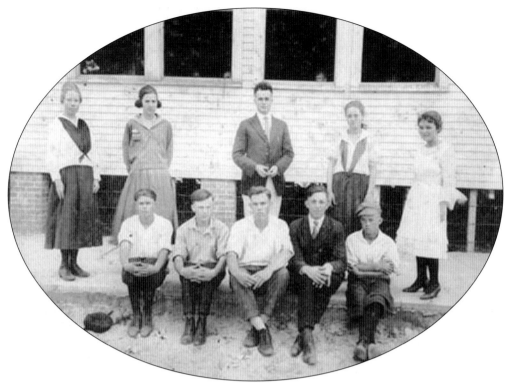

This class at St. Andrews School (undated) was, from left to right, (seated) Lester Pratt, Ernest Spiva, Cecil Surber, Julian Webb, and Melvin Beck; (standing) Pearl Surber, unidentified, Professor Yon, and two unidentified. (SF.)

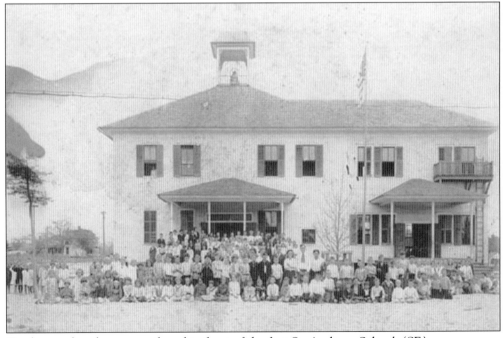

Teachers and students are gathered in front of the first St. Andrews School. (SF.)

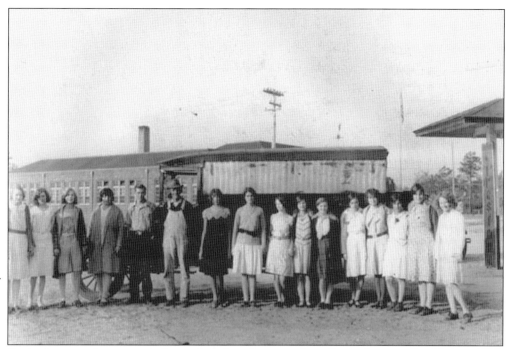

St. Andrews students pose in front of the bus that went from St. Andrews to Bay High in 1928. H. L. Grant was the driver. Shown from left to right are Maude Day, Frances Moates, Phoebe Masker, Ruby Davis Baggett, Fred Moates, H. L. Grant, Hazel Porter, Flossie Warren, Iris Harrison, Henrietta Montgomery, Beatrice Moore, Grace Roache, Maggie Maloy, Evelyn Maddox, Elma Surber, and Muriel Jones. (RM.)

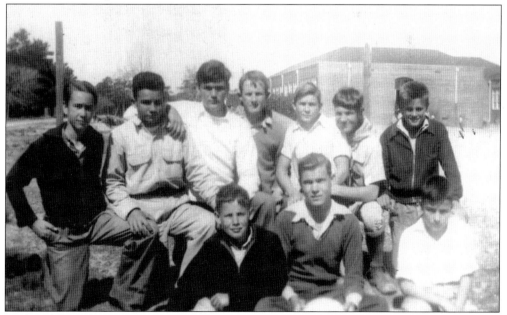

Gathered for a photograph outside St. Andrews School in 1932 are, from left to right, (first row) Lynn Harbeson, Lester Welch, and Jewel Kent; (second row) Guy Baker, Dempsey Kent, Ralph Williams, H. B. Hayes, J. T. Locke, James Peterson, and George Gainer. (MJTL.)

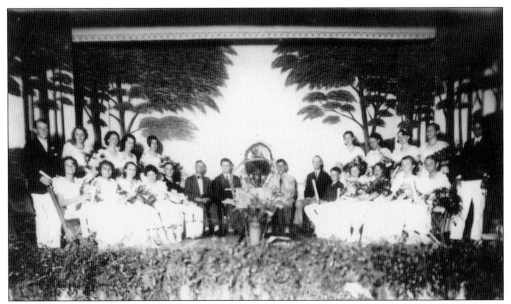

The eighth-grade graduating class at St. Andrews School is shown in 1933. Included here are (seated) Mary Lee Davis, Grace Stephens Helms, Kathryn Gainer Mosier, Gail Miley Fay, A. B. Baker, Josephine Jansenius, Lois Ware Matthews, Bert Ella Warren Drew, Iduma Ellis, and Randall Gwaltney; (standing) Alvin Webb, Lilla Post Dama, Burnell Rutherford, Daisy Lee Richbourg Englehart, Edna Earl Baldwin Kelly, Carroll Williams, Juanita Dykes, Victoria Stephens Helms, Sula Mae Malloy Jenkins, and Versie Lee Glass Hilliard. (VSH.)

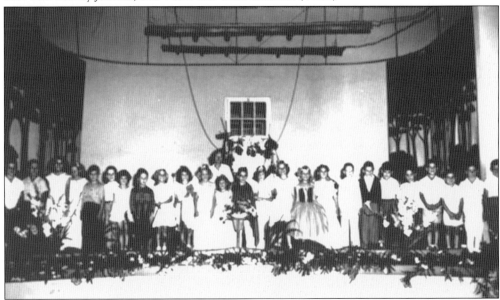

The 1949–1950 second-grade class at St. Andrews School presented a school play. Teacher Mary Post is standing in back. Students are, from left to right, Maurice Cotton, Bobby Martin, Agnes Laramore, Ida Ruth Switzer, Jimmy Fuller, Lawrence Mahoney, Marie Zediker, Jeff Tucker, Shirley McNeal, Lorene Aaron, Joann Cowan, Karen Ann Davis, Johnny Mills, unidentified, Janice Anglin, Martha Hollingshead, Anita Gleitsman, unidentified, Larry McGill, Walter Hobbs, James "Blackie" Mitchell, Ricky Brooks, Arthur Zediker, Billy Grubbs, and Jimmy Zediker. (AGL.)

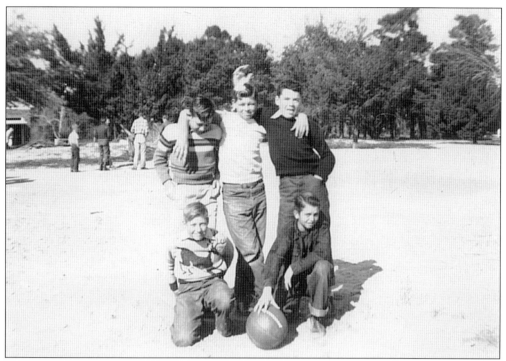

On the playground at St. Andrews School in 1948–1949 are, from left to right, (kneeling) Sammy Moates and Kenneth Kinray; (standing) Rutherford Surber, Jack McKinney, and Leo Baggett. (AJR.)

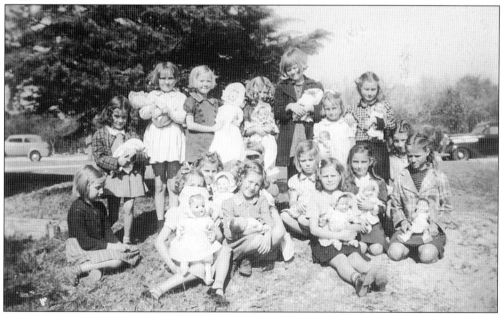

The girls in Mary Post's second-grade class of 1943–1944 brought their dolls to school for this picture. They include Betty Jane Price, Wanda M. Hutchins, Mary M. Fiddler, Laura L. Peel, Mary E. Hoskins, Irma R. Johnson, Marjorie Roche, Odelio Roche, Billy F. Boyt, Kate Watkins, Maggie ?, Kathleen E. Stephens, Joan Peel, Jeanne Retherford, and Lenora Windham. (LWHW.)

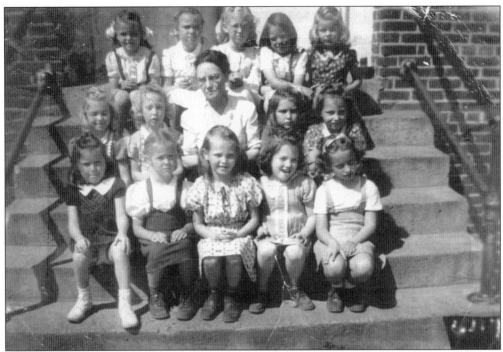

First-grade girls at St. Andrews Elementary School in 1946 gathered on the steps for this photograph. They are, from left to right, (first row) Sylvia Culverhouse, unidentified, Jo Dell Tiller, and two unidentified; (second row) two unidentified, Bessie Bowen (teacher), Estelle Surber, and Sheila Leto; (third row) unidentified, Pat Bridges, Ellafair Bjorklund, and two unidentified. (JDTB.)

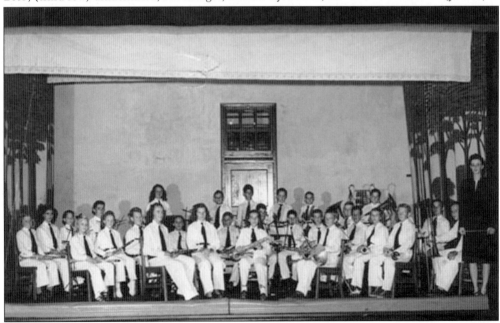

Pictured is the St. Andrews School Band in 1947. Among the band members are Jerry Sowell, Lenora Windham Holman, Albert Rowell, Joe Swann, Alice Bludsworth, Janette Cook, and Wanda Merle Hutchison. (JFS.)

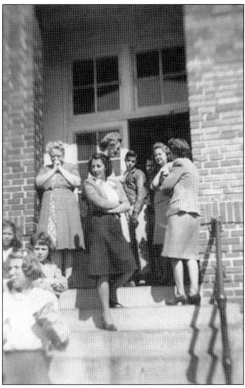

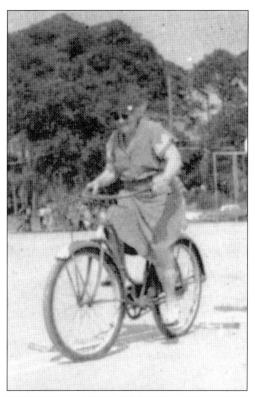

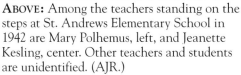

ABOVE: Among the teachers standing on the steps at St. Andrews Elementary School in 1942 are Mary Polhemus, left, and Jeanette Kesling, center. Other teachers and students are unidentified. (AJR.)

ABOVE RIGHT: Martha "Patty" Pilcher could be seen riding her bike around St. Andrews. She never drove a car but always rode her bicycle. Shown here in 1963–1964, she entered the Bicycle Rodeo at the school— and won. Her grandson John E. Pilcher III said, "She even beat me." (BCPL.)

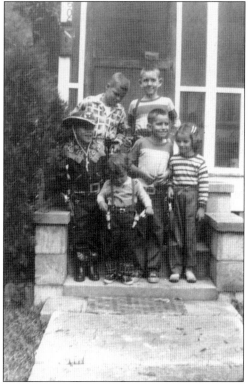

RIGHT: Karen Graham and friends playing cowboys pose for a picture on the steps of the home at 3606 West Sixteenth Street. Karen Graham is in front. Len Eaton is far left in the second row; Duane Graham is left in the third row. (DE.)

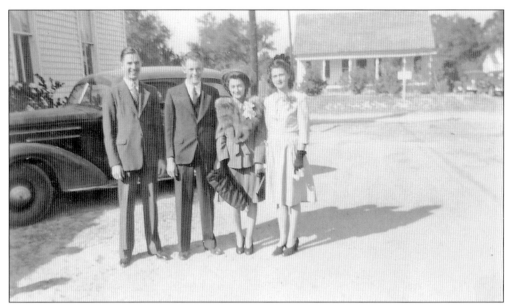

On their wedding day, October 29, 1943, John Thomas (J. T.) Duncan Jr., and his bride, Margaret Anderson Duncan, pose for photographs with their best man, Isaac Cockerham (left), and matron of honor, Bernice Anderson Pratt (right), outside the old St. Andrews Baptist Church. Dr. ? Rogers was the pastor of the church at the corner of Deer Avenue and Fifteenth Street. (MAD.)

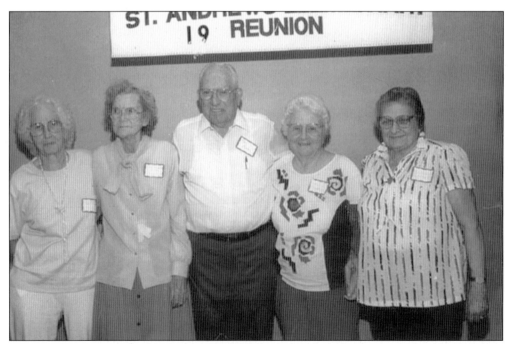

On May 22, 1992, at the St. Andrews School Reunion, these former students gathered for a picture. They are, from left to right, Gussie Groom, age 82; Anna Mae Masker, 91; Ray Moates, 82; Maud Arnold, 83; and unidentified, 82. (RM.)

Four

WARE TOWN

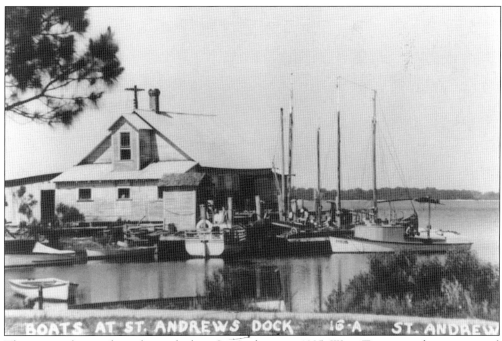

This tranquil view shows boats dock at St. Andrews in 1935. Ware Town was the commercial district of the area. (BCPL)

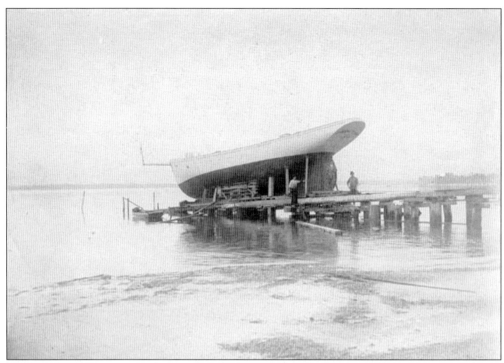

Boat ways were common sights around the bay, as boats had to be pulled out periodically for maintenance and repairs. Two men are shown working on a boat that is on the way. (GMW.)

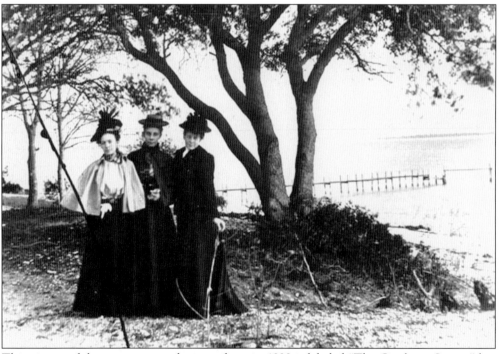

This picture of three women on the waterfront in 1898 is labeled "The Gwaltney Sisters," but their first names are not given. (HJ.)

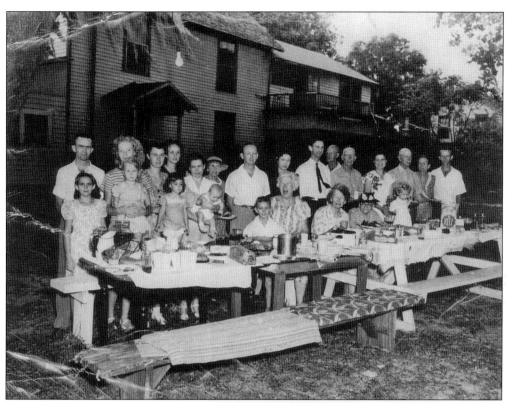

A 1946 Ware family reunion shows (first row) Sarah, Margie, Shirley, Jessie, unidentified, Pearl, two unidentified, and Judy; (second row) Clarence Jr., Helen, Amie, unidentified, Gladys, Sarah Anderson, unidentified, Viloa, Max, Curtis, Clarence Sr., Pallie, Otway, unidentified, and Frank. (SG.)

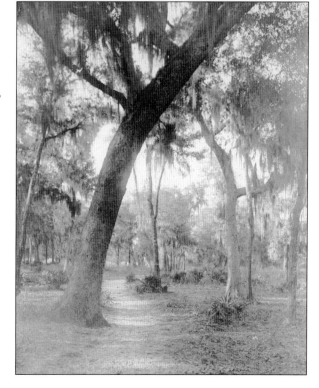

This trail ran through St. Andrews during the mid-1800s. Scenes such as this disappeared with the advancement of settlers and the development of roads. (GMW.)

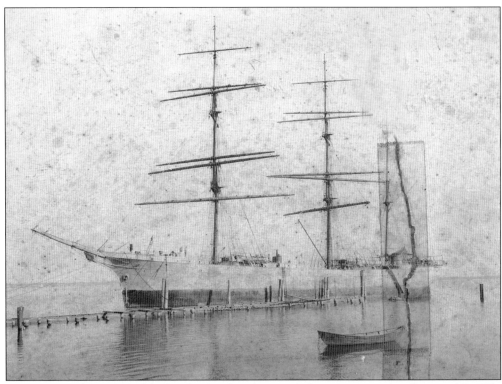

A two-masted ship is docked at the wharf in this photograph from G. M. West's collection. (GMW.)

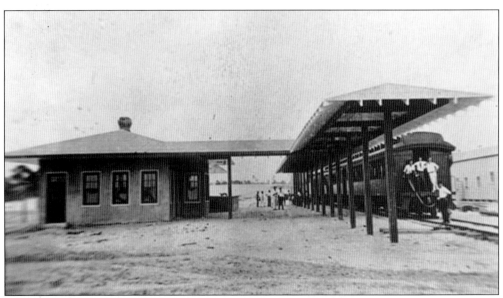

The St. Andrews Bay Railroad terminal was located between Eleventh and Twelfth Streets. On the train, called the "Gallberry Express," tourists would travel from Dothan to St. Andrews. The rail also connected the St. Andrews Ice Plant and docks to the inland. The company considered closing the St. Andrews spur in the 1920s, and Walter C. Sherman, feuding with Lillian West, supported the ultimate closure. (BCPL.)

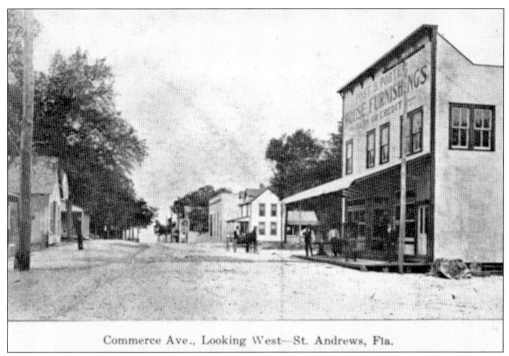

Commerce Ave., Looking West—St. Andrews, Fla.

This *c.* 1900 postcard of a photograph by E. W. Masker shows Commerce Avenue looking west. The sign painted on the front of the building on the right says "Post and Porter house furnishings cash or credit." (BCPL.)

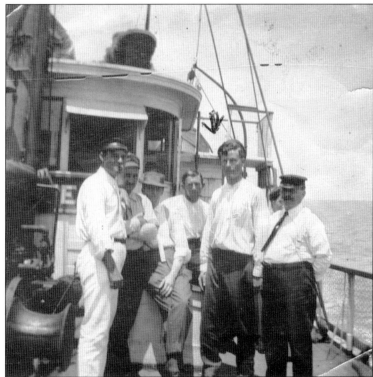

Henry Munson, second from right, was a master merchant seaman who had a license to sail anywhere in the world. He was licensed to bring his vessel into St. Andrews Bay without a pilot. In most cases, the pilot goes out to meet the ship that is coming into the bay and guides it in. (CHM.)

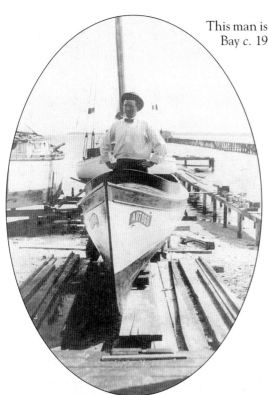

This man is in a newly built boat adjacent to St. Andrews Bay *c.* 1900. The boat was named *Autogo*. (GMW.)

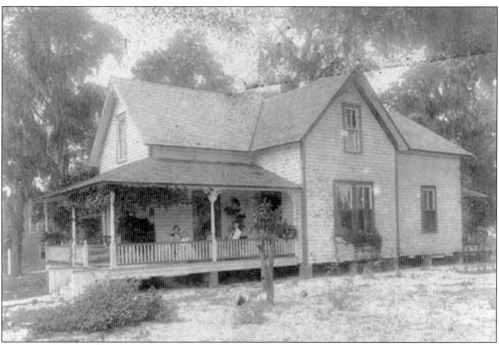

In this 1913 photograph of the home of Ed and Maud Day at 1001 Calhoun Avenue, Mr. and Mrs. Day and daughter Louise are on the porch. Ed Day built the family home in 1909–1910, and in 2007, the fourth generation of the family occupies the home. (EDM.)

On the porch of the Day home are, from left to right, Margaret Louise Day, Maud Ellen Day Leto, and Maud Gainer Day. (SLS.)

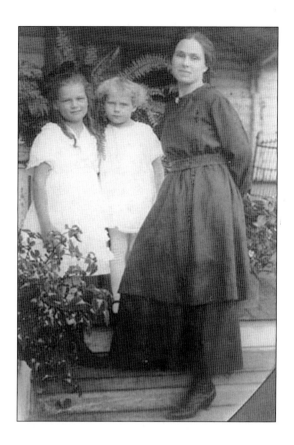

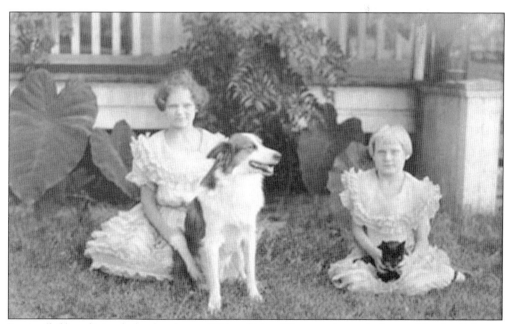

Louise (left) and Maud, the daughters of Ed and Maud Day, are shown in front of the family home with their dog and cat c. 1916–1920. (EDM.)

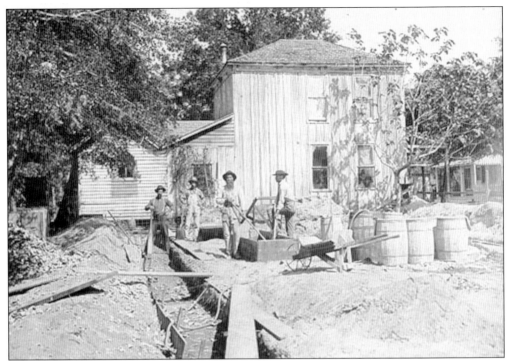

The Bank of St. Andrews was under construction in 1906–1907. Workmen pictured here are, from left to right, Sam Surber, George Surber, Adam Levi Welch, and June Welch. The building, located on the corner of Beck Avenue and Tenth Street, was used as a substation of the Panama City Police Department from 1997 to 2005. It was purchased by Coastal Community Bank in 2006 and restored. (BCPL.)

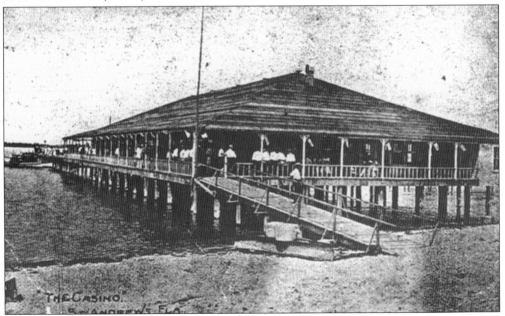

The casino pictured was the U.S. Port of Entry built and owned by C. C. Gedion. It was located in the bay at the foot of Thirteenth Street in St. Andrews. (RM.)

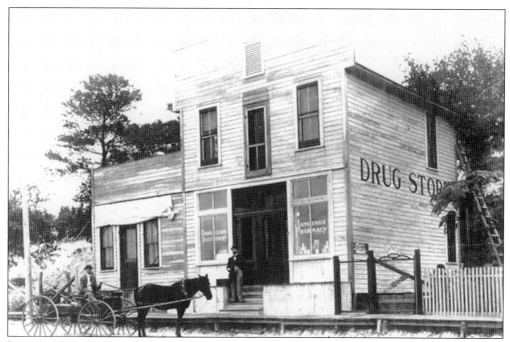

Jansenius Drug Store is shown in 1916 on Commerce Avenue, which is now Tenth Street in St. Andrews. (RM.)

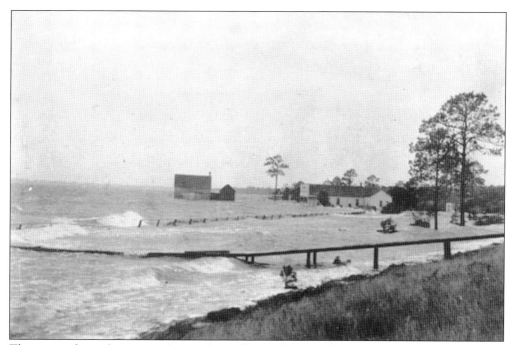

This image shows damage to the wooden walkway along the beach in St. Andrews; high water damage is the result of a hurricane in 1900. (BCPL.)

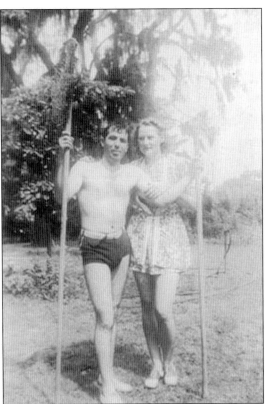

Bruno Frank Leto and Maud Leto seem to be on the way to the bay in this 1930 photograph. (SLS.)

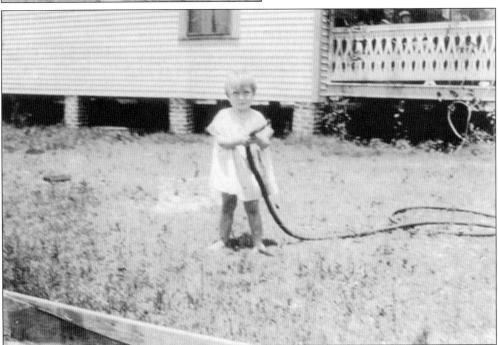

Gertrude Day, the daughter of Ed and Maud Day, is playing with a water hose in front of aunt Sarah Elizabeth Gainer Gwaltney home c. 1920. (EDM.)

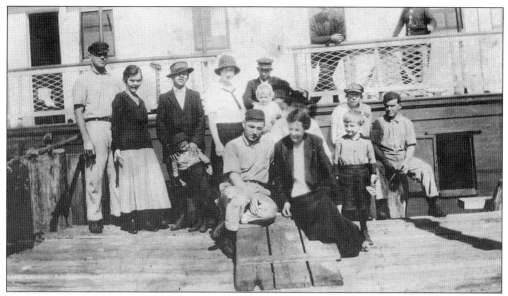

This group of people is in front of the steamer *Tarpon* in 1935. The two men on the boat are unidentified. From left to right in the first row are Nix Ellis and Ethel Purcell (seated), and Newton Ware (standing). The rest of the group included Huey Cobb, chief on the *Tarpon*; Willie Pope; Hugh Ellis; Pearl Ellis (Ware); Hansel Ellis; baby Selma Ellis (Kohler); Dell Ellis; Ollie Ellis (Walker); and Cliff Cobb, who worked on the *Tarpon*. (JDTB.)

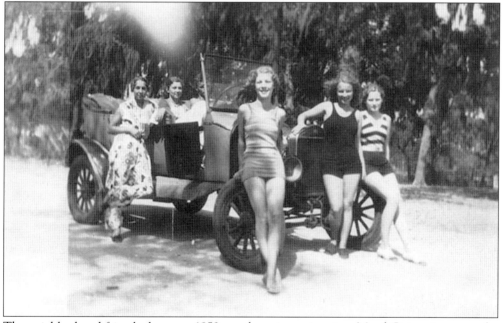

The neighborhood friends shown *c.* 1950 may be going swimming. Maud Gainer is among the group, according to notes. (SLS.)

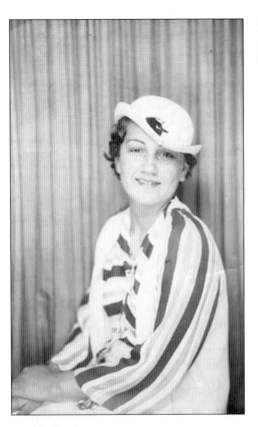

Here is a photograph of Margaret Gainer from the photograph collection of the Leto family. (SLS.)

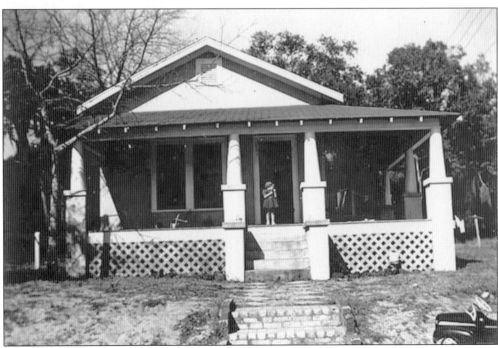

Sheila Leto is shown on the front porch of the family home at 2204 West Ninth Street. (SLS.)

Sheila Leto is shown in August 1941 sitting on the back of a car. The St. Andrews water tower can be seen at left in the background. (SLS.)

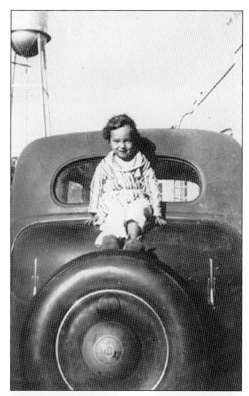

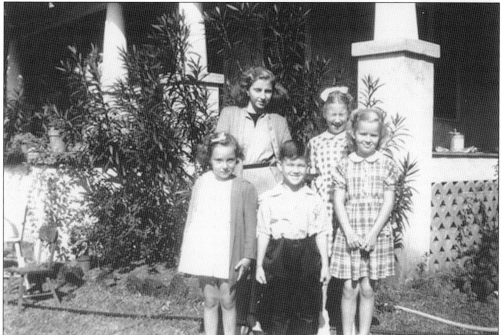

These friends, who all lived in the same neighborhood, are in front of the Leto home at 2204 West Ninth Street. They are, from left to right, (first row) Sheila Day Leto, Donnie Thomas, and Dorothy Cook; (second row) Gainell Gainer and Cynthia Ruth Maxon. (SLS.)

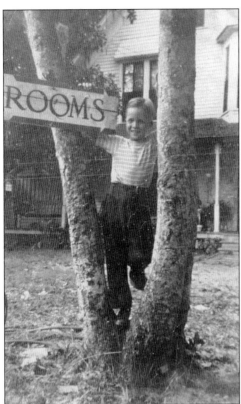

Albert Rowell and his family moved to St. Andrews in the late 1930s and lived on Ninth Street near Truesdell Park. Albert is pictured here in the yard. (AJR.)

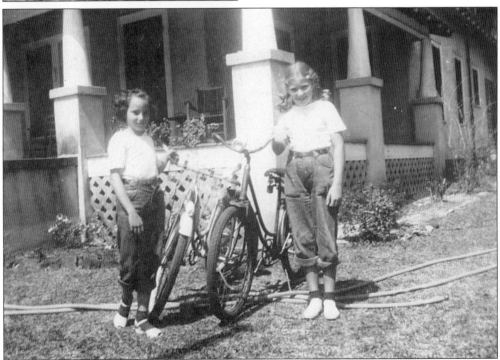

Sheila Leto (left) and Freida Whitchard are ready to go bike riding. (SLS.)

Pictured in 1940 are cousins Cynthia Maxon, Freida Whitchard, and Sheila Leto, "in Chuck's car," according to the back of the photograph. (SLS.)

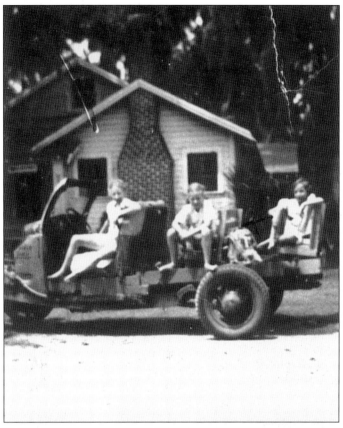

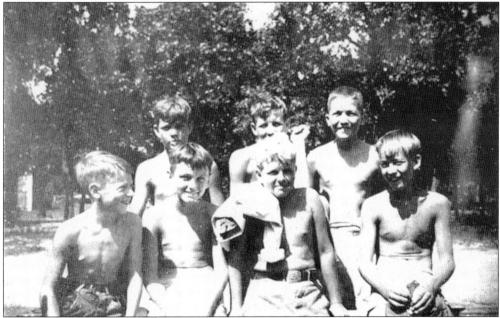

These St. Andrews friends posing for a photograph c. 1945 are, from left to right, Fred Moates, Jack Laird, Bill Rowell, Edwin Peters, unidentified, Bud Arnold, and Hoke Grant. (AJR.)

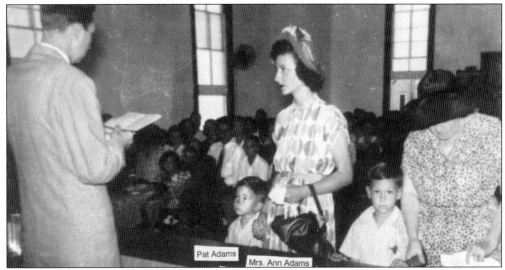

A baptism ceremony in 1950 included, from left to right, Reverend Bradley, Pat Adams, Ann Adams (Pat and Mike's mother), Mike Adams, and Jane Adams (Pat and Mike's grandmother). Until 1955, St. Andrews Methodist Church was located at 1004 Chestnut Avenue. In 2006–2007, Historic St. Andrew Church acquired a historic preservation grant from the Florida Department of State Bureau of Historic Preservation to restore the sanctuary, which was originally constructed in 1887. Notice the open windows and fan mounted on the window frame for cooling the room. (HSAC.)

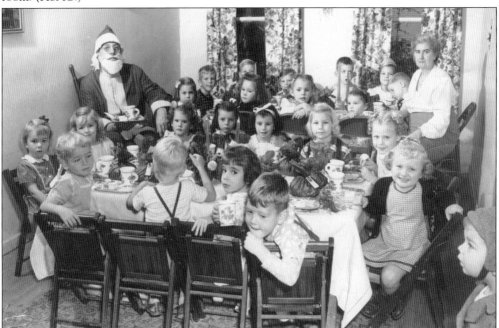

St. Andrews Methodist Church kindergarten is shown in the 1947 Christmas party. Mrs. B. I. Hughen was the teacher. Students seated around tables include Bobby Martin, Bobby Raffield, Josh Vann, Gloria Jean Holman, Marie Zediker, Brenda Joyce Keim, Gloria Jean Floyd, Betty Ruth Paysinger, Carolyn Cook, Janice Anglin, Claudia McDonald, Gloria Dawn Hold, Linda Jo Gardner, and Aubrey Cooper Littleton. (BM.)

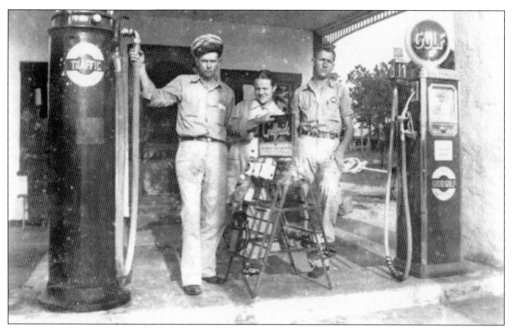

The Gulf Oil Station on Beck Avenue is shown in an undated photograph with Newell Arnold (left), Ann Arnold (center), and unidentified. (MAB.)

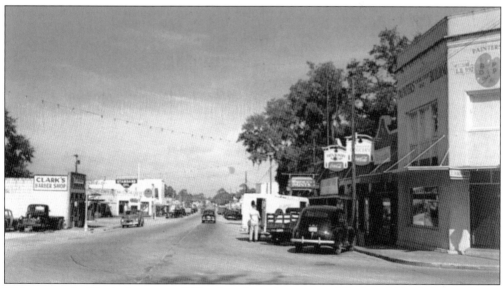

This postcard of Beck Avenue c. 1940, taken from the corner of Beck and Tenth Street, shows, from left to right, Clark's Barber Shop, Standard Oil Gas Station, St. Andrews Grocery, Pat's Sundry Shop, Ward Hardware Company, and the Brotherhood of Painters, Decorators, and Paper Hangers of America, Local 992. (BCPL.)

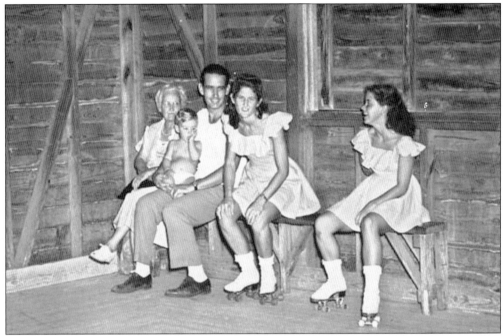

It was Mary Dyer's birthday in 1947, and her party was held at the skating rink. Attending are, from left to right, Mrs. Tucker, Frank Dyer holding Frank Dyer Jr., Mary Dyer, and Peggy Cotton. (MTD.)

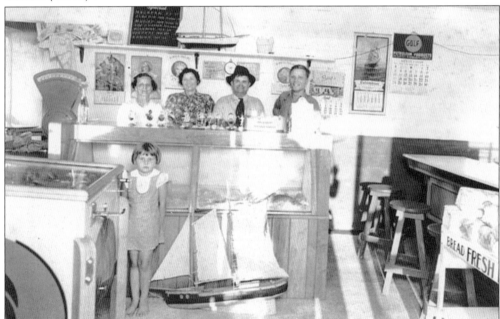

Windham's Fish and Ice, at 1119 Beck Avenue, is shown in April 1938. In the fish market and oyster bar are, pictured from left to right, (in front) Lenora Windham; (behind the counter) Tannie Windham, Rena Dell Windham, Aaron T. Windham, and Tony Windham. Today Lenora's son Mitch and his wife, Carolyn, run the Captains Table Restaurant and Oyster Bar in this same location. (LWHW.)

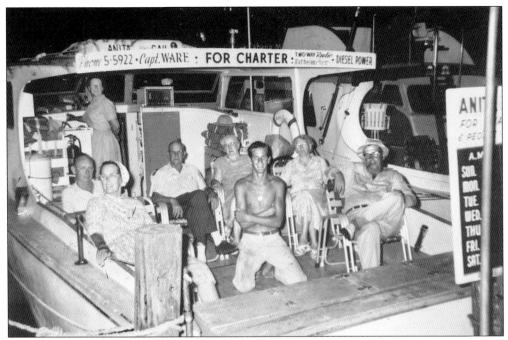

A fishing party is shown in 1940 on the boat *Anita Gail*, docked at the Smith Yacht Basin. Notes on the picture state: "Capt. Curtis Ware [sitting in the chair in the center and his wife Pearl Ellis sitting next to him] Family members on the boat are Elzie Ellis [Tiller], Newton Ware, Selma Ellis [Kohler], John Kohler, Kina Ellis [Newman] and a deck hand." (JDTB.)

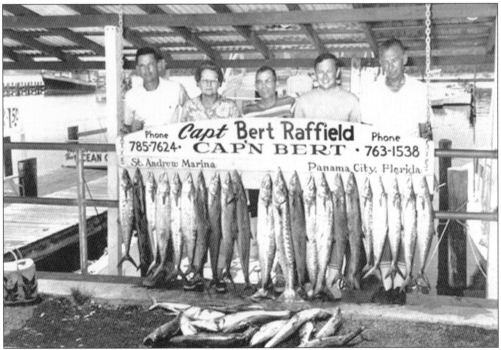

A party of five, fishing with Capt. Bert Raffield, shows off their catch of the day on June 28, 1969, in this photograph by Harold Gornall. (SLS.)

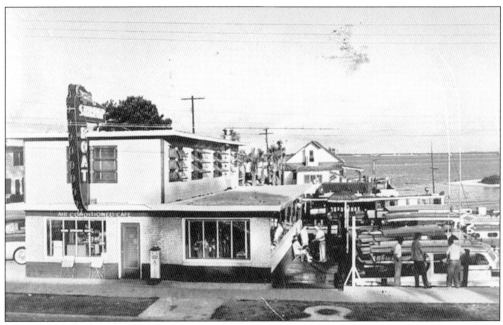

The Shrimp Boat Restaurant, on Beck Avenue next to Smith's Yacht Basin, was constructed and opened in 1950. A notice above the door points out that it is an "Air Conditioned Cafe." The peaked roof of the fish house can be seen in the background. (BCPL.)

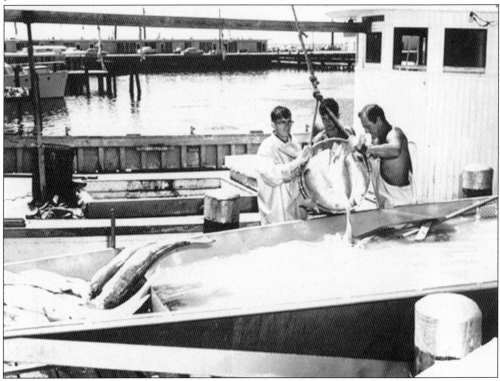

Fishermen are shown loading fish into a holding box in the 1960s at St. Andrews. Marina shops can be seen in the background. (BCPL.)

Joel Lucas is behind the counter in the retail part of St. Andrews Fish Market in the 1950s. Lucas worked at the fish market for about 27 years when Calvin Smith owned it, and in 1982, he became owner/operator, continuing until his death in 1992. (JL.)

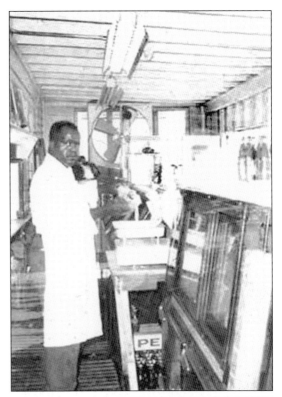

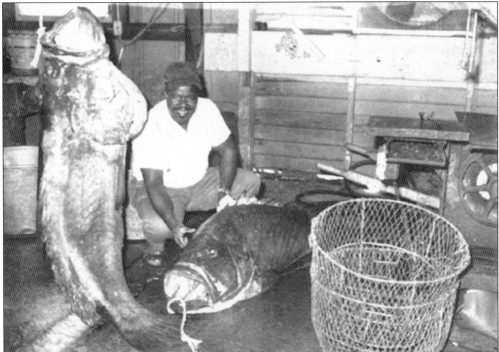

Joel Lucas is shown processing some large fish at the fish market at 3309 West Twelfth Street in St. Andrews in the 1950s. (JL.)

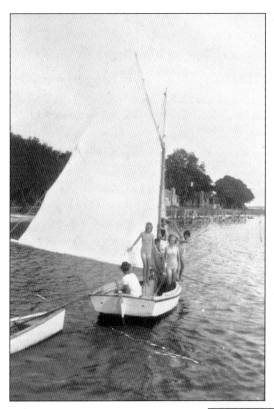

This sailboat, pictured in 1942, is heading for Buena Vista Point to pick up scallops. The beach between the trees is off Tenth and Eleventh Streets. On the boat are Lillian Spinks and her children, Roy Jr. and Elizabeth Ann; Willie and Bea Findley standing in back of the boat; and Chester Adam Welch, seated. (BMO.)

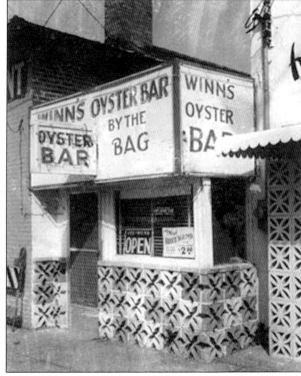

Winn's Oyster Bar was attached to the south side of the Panama City Publishing Building on Beck Avenue and was originally constructed as a small apartment for an employee at the publishing company sometime in the 1930s. (GMW.)

Beginning in 1953, Bill Tant's Southern Skin Divers Supply in Birmingham, Alabama, scheduled regular diving trips to St. Andrews. In 1960, Bill and his wife, Eloise, purchased the home at 3014 West Eleventh Street, across from St. Andrews Marina. There they housed divers on army cots, getting up early in the mornings to take a charter boat to the SS *Tarpon* wreck, Stage 1, Simpson, and other sites in the Gulf to dive. John Wengel, standing 6 foot 3 inches, is pictured here at age 18 in 1961, standing in front of the house with a bow anchor from the SS *Tarpon*. (BT.)

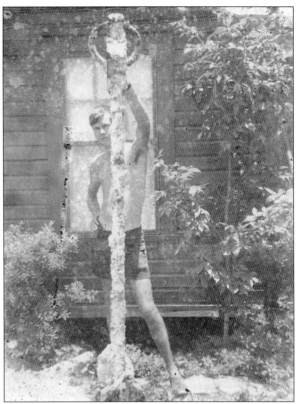

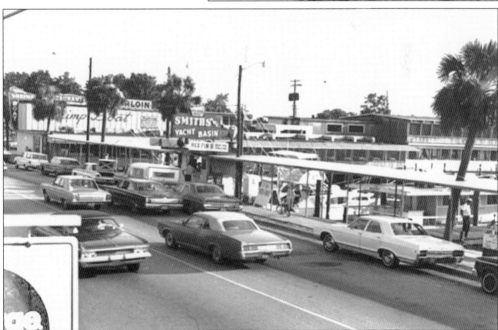

Parking space seems scarce in this Bob Hargis photograph of traffic in the 1970s by the Smith's Yacht Basin. It was a popular place to book a fishing trip. The Shrimp Boat Restaurant can be seen in the background. (BCPL.)

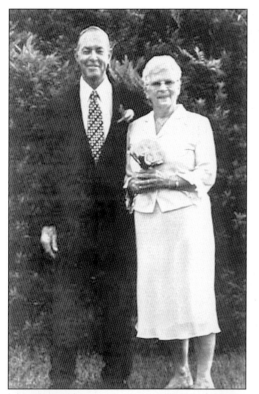

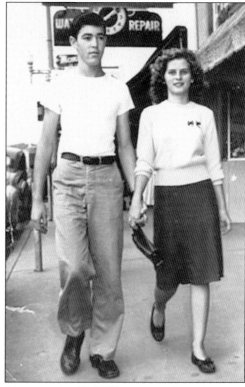

ABOVE LEFT: Dick Warriner and Lenora Windham Holman Warriner are shown on their wedding day, August 29, 2006. (LWHW.)

ABOVE: In 1948, St. Andrews residents Dick Warriner and Lenora Windham stroll down Palafox Street on a visit to Pensacola, Florida. The high school friends were reunited and became husband and wife in 2006. (LWHW.)

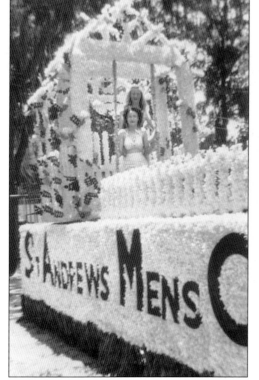

LEFT: Helen Ware, in back, and Inez Ellis (Kozlowsky), in front, ride the St. Andrews Men's Club float in a parade c. 1944. (BCPL.)

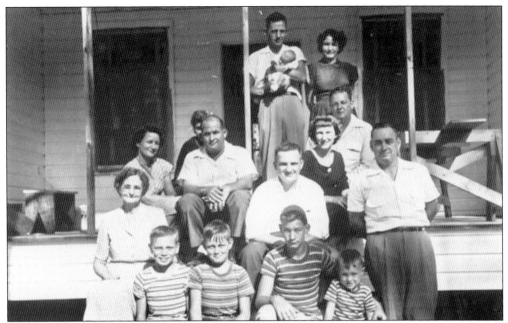

This family portrait was taken on the steps of the home of Ethel Ellis, 2609 West Eleventh Street, in the 1950s. Included from left to right are (first row) Benny Lister, Roy Lister, Clyde Davis, and Frank Kozlowsky; (second row) Ethel Mason (Ellis), Joe Stravinski, and Clyde Ellis; (third row) Estelle Ellis (Davis), Perry Davis, and Maxie Ellis (Lister); (fourth row) Iduma Ellis (Stravinski) (behind Perry Davis), and R. D. Lister; (fifth row) Ted Kozlowsky, Inez Ellis (Kozlowsky), and baby Cindy Kozlowsky. Clyde Ellis, son of Ethel Ellis, worked as a printer for the *Panama City Pilot* before going to work for the *Panama City News Herald.* (JDTB.)

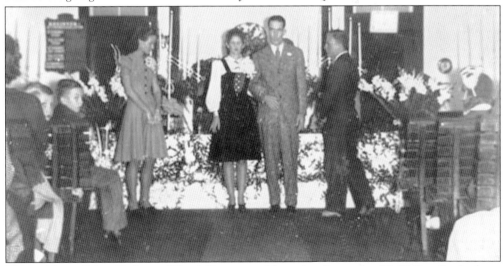

The wedding of Mary Tucker and Frank Dyer was celebrated on September 28, 1940, at St. Andrews Methodist Church on Chestnut Avenue and Eleventh Street. From left to right are Albert Rowell, Bill Rowell, Louise Smith, Mary Tucker, Frank Dyer, and Leslie Smith. Fay LaGallee was the pianist. This is a Masker photograph. On the back of the picture is written: "The church was decorated by the women of the church. The building had been remodeled on the inside. The old wood heater used to stand in front of Frank and I." (MTD.)

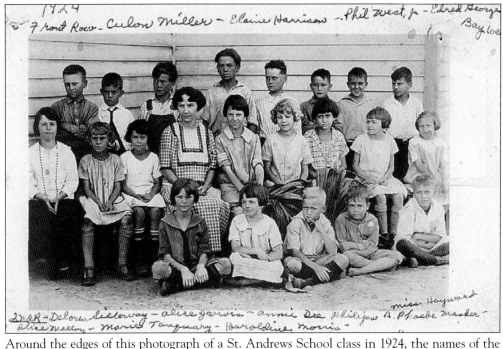

Around the edges of this photograph of a St. Andrews School class in 1924, the names of the teacher and students were written. They are, from left to right, (first row) Culon Miller, Elaine Harrison, Phil West Jr., Edred George, and Bay West; (second row) Deloris Silloway, Alice Jarvis, Pearl Grooms, teacher Violet Haywood, Annie Dee Phillips, Phoebe Estelle Masker, Alice Maloy, Marie Tanquary, and Haroldene Morris; (third row) Glenn Porter, Donal Wright, Louie Weaver, Theo Horton, Lloyd Coram, Jake Haugh, Gibson Lowe, and Arthur Titus. (BCPL.)

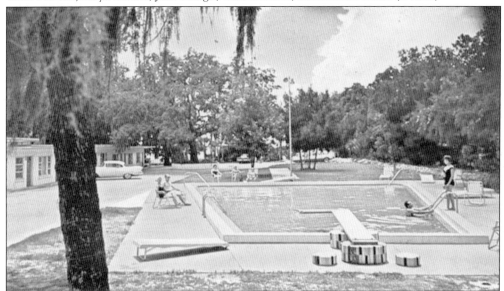

A postcard shows the pool at Scenic Motor Court in 1953. The motel was on Route 98 overlooking the bay on Buena Vista Point (West Tenth Street and Beck Avenue). In 1995, the City of Panama City acquired the land and designated it as a public park, Oaks by the Bay Park, and preserved the large oak tree seen in the background. (JG.)

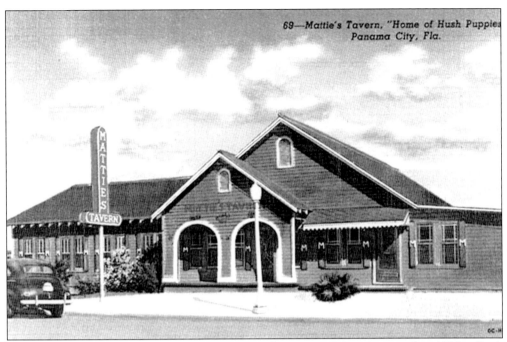

This postcard says Mattie's Tavern, "Home of Hush Puppies." Mattie's opened in 1936 at Beck Avenue and Twelfth Street. It closed about 1959. (BCPL.)

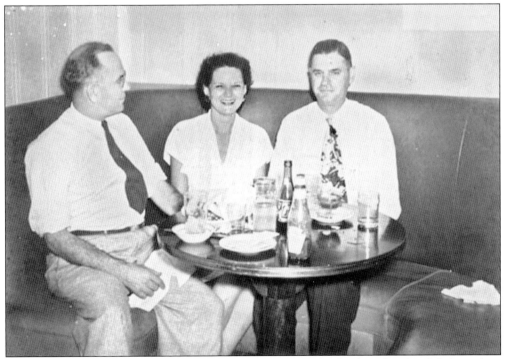

In 1946, Louise Day was photographed with her husband, Claude Whitchard, left, and an unidentified man at a table in Mattie's Tavern (EDM.)

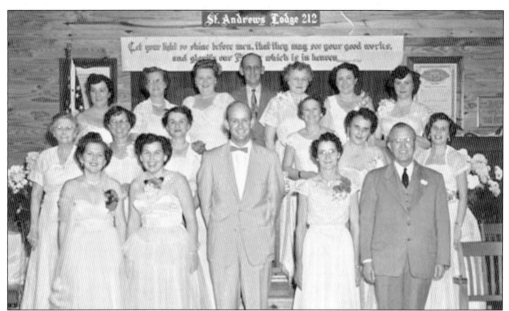

St. Andrews Lodge 212 of the Eastern Star is shown in this undated photograph. Those attending include, from left to right, (first row) Marion Walsingham, Irene Carter, Milton Carter, Winnie ?, and unidentified; (second row) four unidentified, Esther Johnson, and Lenora Windham; (third row) two unidentified, Delores Welburn, three unidentified, ? Howard, and Ann Hutchison. (LWHW.)

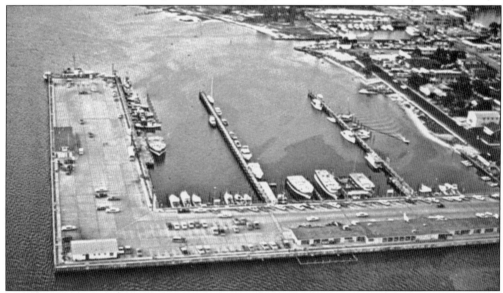

This aerial view of St. Andrews Marina is from a postcard that states: "One block off Highway 98 . . . deep sea fishing boats, charter boats for private trips, a fish market, tackle shop, souvenirs, barber shop, lounge, newsstand and seafood restaurant." St. Andrews Marina has evolved over the years, first being a wooden dock known as Ware's Wharf, where ships and boats unloaded supplies for sale at Ware's Mercantile. The wooden dock was later used more for recreational fishing. In 1960, the City of Panama City constructed the St. Andrews Marina, where commercial and recreational fishing thrived. The city refurbished the marina with floating docks and amenities in 2002. (BCPL.)

Five

WEST END

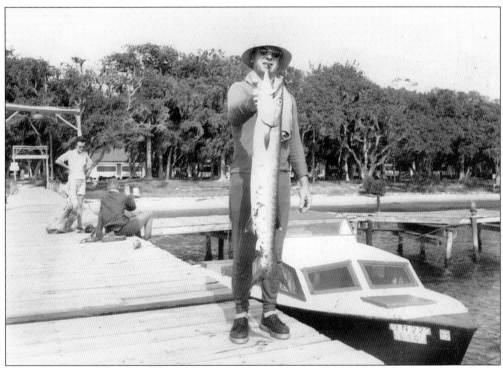

Dave Abts from Birmingham, Alabama, is standing on the dock at Baywood Court, vacation cabins located between Port Panama City and the Hathaway Bridge. He is showing off a barracuda he speared in the Gulf of Mexico (c. 1960). However, a more stunning find for Abts was during the time coming in from a dive trip that he had the boat captain drop him near the port so he could scuba back to Baywood. When he reached the beach, he realized his wedding ring had come off; he retraced his path and found the ring on the bottom. (BT.)

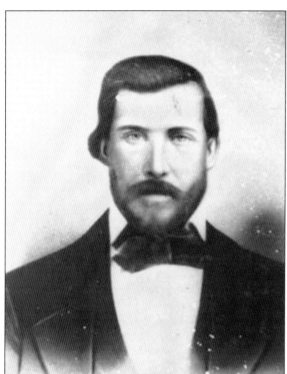

Francis Merrion Moates was born June 14, 1837, and married Mary Peel on March 31, 1859. Their children were William Noah, Mary Frances, Emma Ellen, James Augustus, Andrew Marion, Benjamin Franklin, Carrie E. and Noah Webster (twins), John Bunyan, Columbus Perry, and Annie Caster. (RM.)

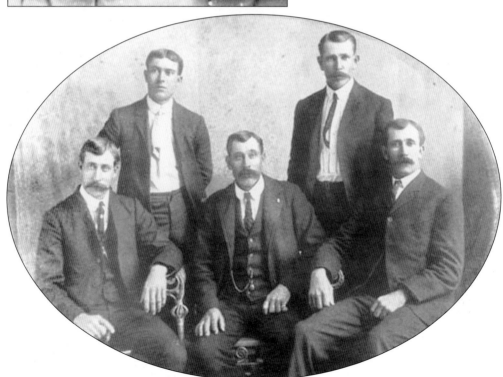

Five of Francis and Mary Moates's sons are pictured here. They are, from left to right "Bun," Lum, Noah, Ben, and James Merrion. (RM.)

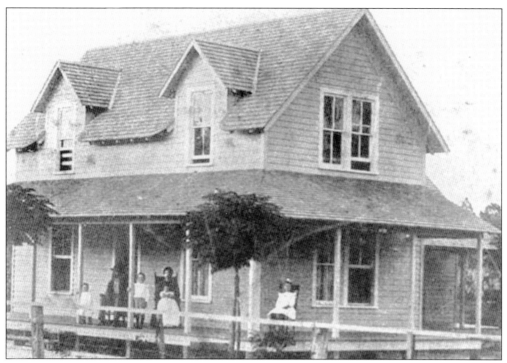

In the 1880s, Francis Moates owned several acres in West End, south of Nineteenth Street and between Michigan and Hannah Avenues. Moates operated a sawmill at the south end of Danford Avenue and most likely built this home with pine from the mill. (RM.)

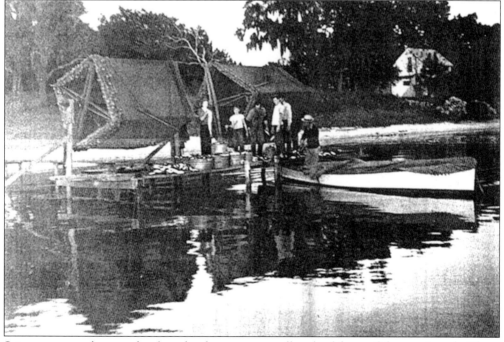

Seine nets, a net boat, and reels to dry the nets on are all tools of the net fisherman's trade. These are in front of the Moates home. Note the mullet on the dock. (RM.)

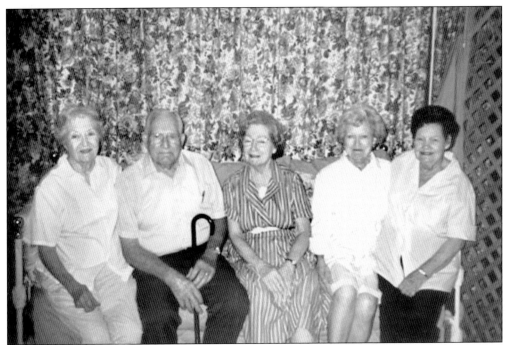

The children of Lum and Nettie Moates, pictured on August 11, 1996, are, from left to right, Frances Moates Bukota, Ray Moates, Marjorie Moates Ware, Betty Moates Burdick, and Henrietta Montgomery Moates (wife of Ray). (RM.)

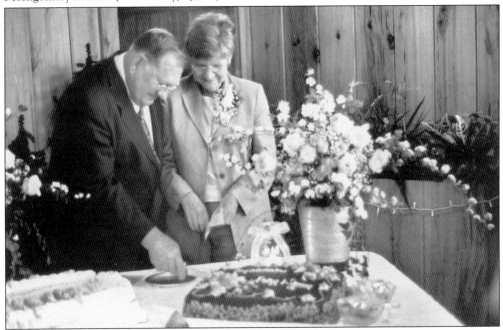

Sammy Moates and Patsy Cosson Moates celebrate their wedding on March 31 just as do Sammy's father, Ray Moates, and grandfather Frances Merrion Moates. Ray's wedding was 73 years to the day after Francis's, and Sam and Patsy's wedding on March 31, 2004, was 72 years to the day after Ray's. (PCM.)

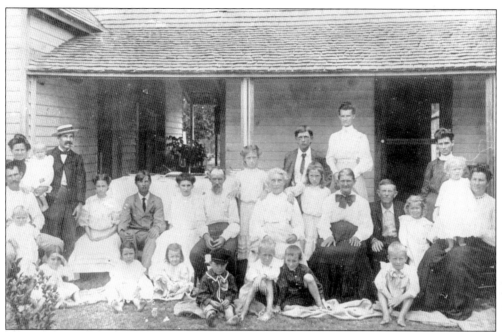

The Ernest Morris family is sitting in front of their house as it originally sat at 1608 Louise Avenue. Ernie and Jesse Morris were married in 1925 and had four children here. Their oldest son, Ernest Isadora "Bubba" Morris, and his wife, Eunice, gave the home to Jim and Doris Pigneri to be moved, preserved, and converted into a restaurant overlooking St. Andrews Marina, where "Uncle Ernie" was known to many and made his livelihood. Doris is the great-niece of Uncle Ernie. Uncle Ernie is pictured seated in the middle. (JDP.)

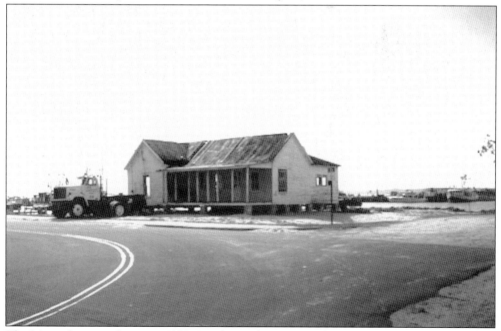

The Morris house is shown in 1993, "on the road" to its new location at 1151 Bayview Avenue and its new life as Uncle Ernie's, which opened in November 1994. (BCPL.)

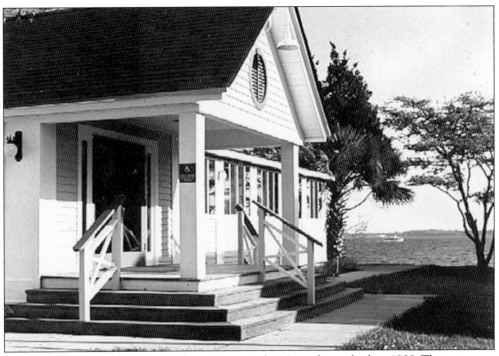

Theo's Restaurant at 4423 West Highway 98 was in the Moates home, built in 1908. The restaurant is now Canopies. (BCPL.)

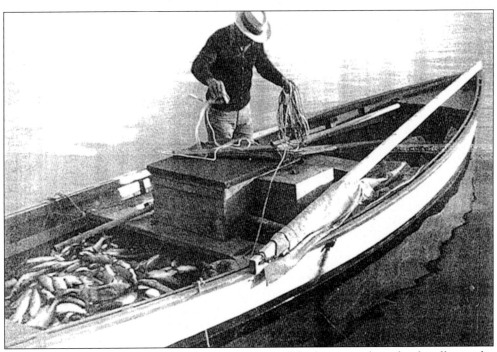

Lum Moates is working on his net boat in 1970—and he has a good catch of mullet in the boat. (RM.)

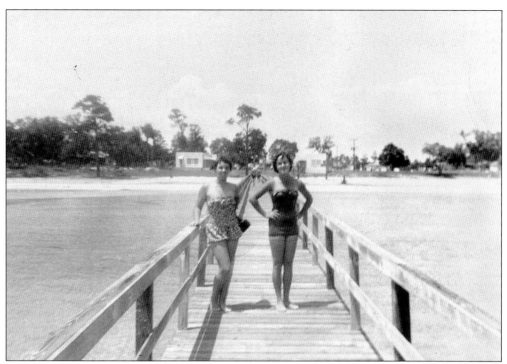

Louise Lowe (left) and Joan Turner pose for a photograph on the dock on the bay at the end of Baltimore Avenue. (TSV.)

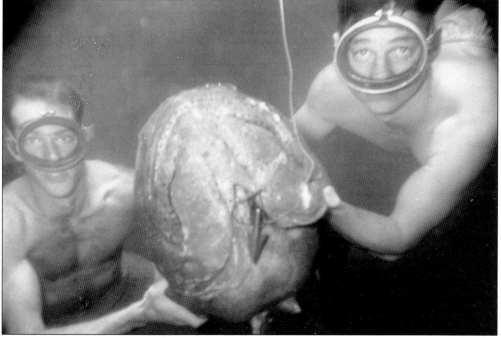

Bill Tant (also known as "Capn Scuba") took many still and underwater pictures in the 1950s and 1960s. Here divers Ray Fincher (left) and Dean Wilkerson show off a 350-pound jewfish that was speared at the twin barges near the inshore tower in about 70 feet of water. (BT.)

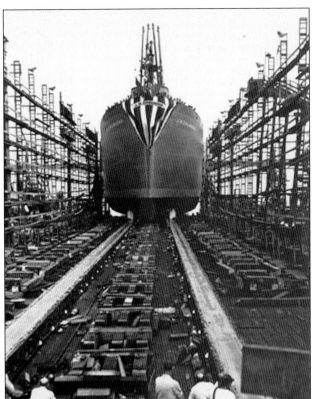

This photograph is of the launching of the Liberty ship *J. H. Drummond* from Wainwright Shipyard. The shipyard in the spring of 1943 began building the Liberty ships that would play a vital role in World War II. Workers streamed into the area to work for "high wages." The shipyard ran three shifts a day. Many of the workers were women, and sometimes husbands and wives both worked at the shipyard. (SLS.)

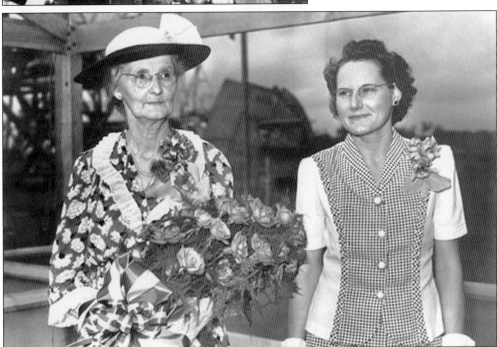

Grace Day Drummond (left) and Maude Day Leto are shown at the launching of the Liberty ship *J. H. Drummond*. Mrs. Drummond was the sponsor of the ship. (SLS.)

Inez Ellis (Kozlowsky), left, and Louise Muse pose with brush and broom in front of the U.S. Post Office where they both worked in 1944. On the window of the building, it says Wainwright Park Station, Panama City, Florida. The Wainwright Park Station Post Office was established February 20, 1943, and discontinued September 15, 1945. (JDTB.)

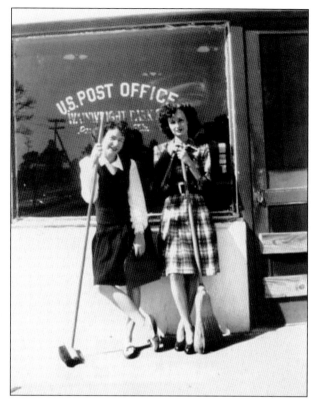

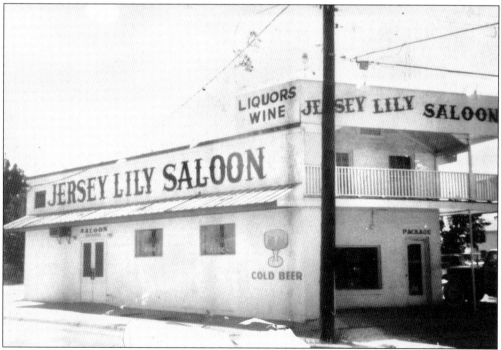

Jersey Lily—located at Highway 98 and Alabama Avenue—later became Inez's Liquor Store and eventually the original home of J Michael's Restaurant. (BCPL.)

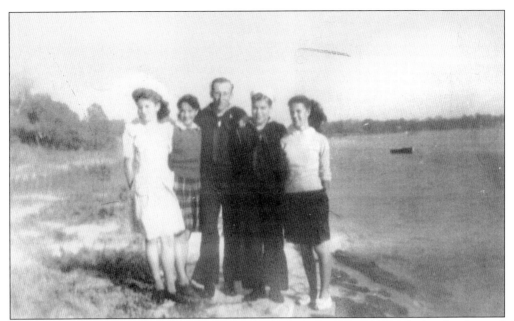

In 1943, the McClard family lived at 1701 Danford Avenue. Mr. McClard worked at the shipyard and had three daughters. He taught them Morse code, and the girls "talked" by flashlight to sailors on ships in the bay. They exchanged addresses and wrote letters. Shown from left to right are Helen McClard, Evelyn McClard, Don Carter, Shorty ?, and Delores McClard. In 2004, Evelyn and her daughter visited St. Andrews and visited with the owner of the house, Kathy Swigler. (KS.)

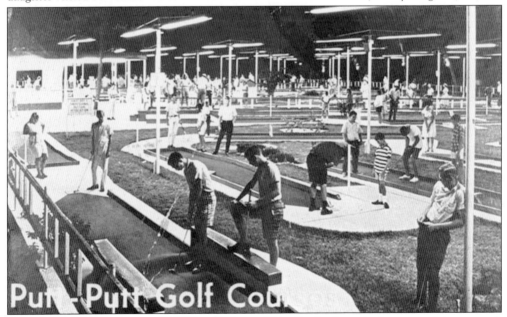

The putt-putt golf course at 4718 West Highway 98 in St. Andrews is shown on this postcard. On the card it says, "America's Quality Putting Course. Present this card for one free game (18 holes)." In the 1961 Panama City Directory, it states that T. A. Tucker, proprietor, advertises, "Spend an evening at miniature golf, bring your family and friends, America's finest, Tel Poplar 3-7171." The course was built by John Gleitsman. (BCPL.)

Six

HENTZ PASTURE

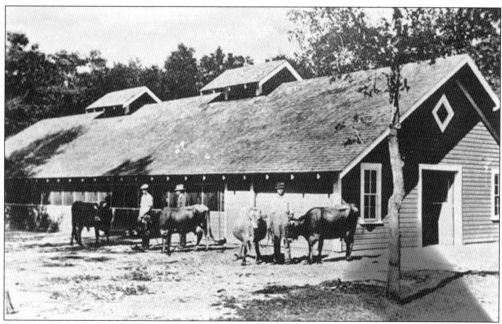

St. Andrew Bay Dairy was started in 1921 by Mr. and Mrs. O. E. Miley, who sold the business to John Hentz in 1942. Hentz was an agricultural agent. He and his wife, Ruth, operated the dairy for 31 years. The property included 417 acres of land, from Nineteenth Street north to Twenty-seventh Street, from Frankford Avenue on the east to Beck Avenue and Pretty Bayou Drive on the west. In 1968, he moved the dairy to Washington County. It had been here 54 years. (JH.)

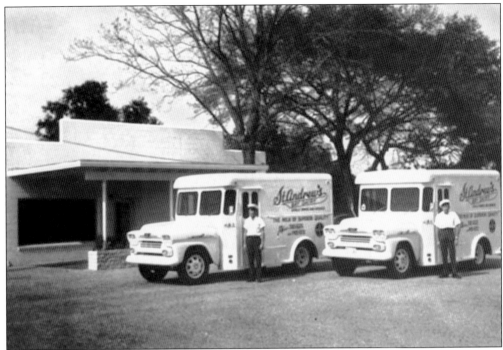

Delivery trucks are ready to go in front of the dairy on Highway 390. The drivers are Wayne George, left, and Jeff Morris. (JH.)

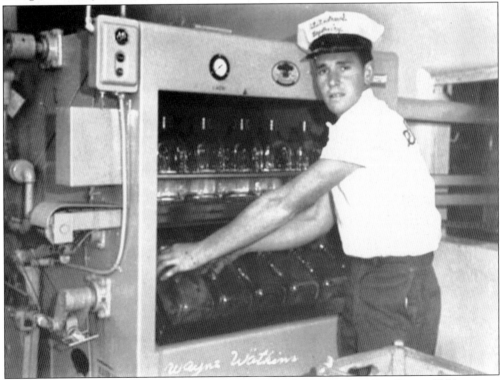

Wayne Watkins is working at the bottling machine in the St. Andrew Bay Dairy. (JH.)

Lewie M. Andrews, right, chats with his brother Chester at a family reunion in Truesdell Park in the early 1950s. Chester moved here for Alabama in the 1940s to work at the shipyard. Lewie brought his family in 1958 and moved into a new house in the new John Hentz subdivision in St. Andrews. A career army officer, he left the family here while serving in Korea, Vietnam, and Germany. (JLA.)

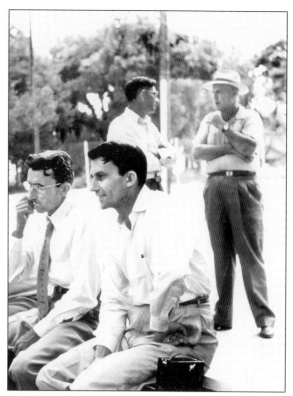

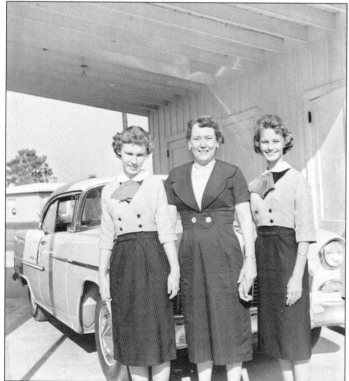

Mary Delma Andrews, flanked by her daughters Judy (left) and Louie (right), was gifted at gardening and sewing. She filled the yard with trees and bushes and made clothes for the girls. The family attended St. Andrews Baptist Church. (JLA.)

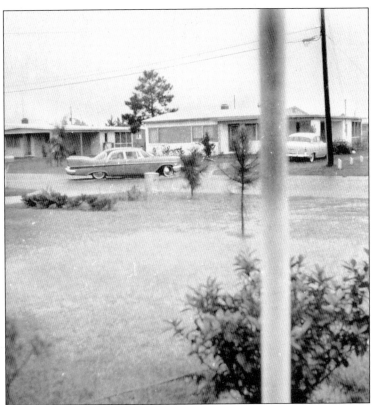

Rainstorms sometimes flooded the pastureland but provided cozy afternoons. John Hentz, in *The Heritage of Bay County I*, said he started developing this area after he established a 910 dairy business in Washington County and moved his cows up there. The area where Tommy Thomas Chevrolet is used to be his cow pasture, he said. Development included Pretty Bayou Heights, additions to St. Andrews Meadowbrook, and a lot of unplatted residential and business property. (JLA.)

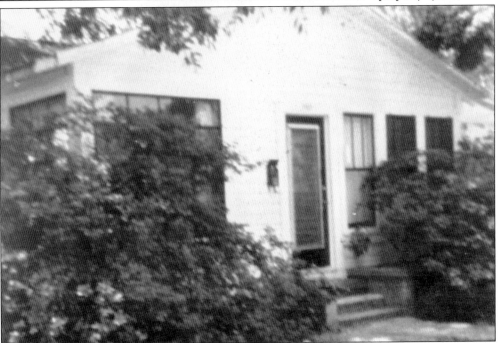

This house at 2901 West Eighteenth Street on the corner of Chestnut Avenue was the home of James and June Rabon and their family. (TRG.)

Present at Jim Rabon's birthday party *c.* 1967 were, from left to right, his sister Faye Gautier, Teresa Rabon, Jim, his sister Judy Gautier, and four friends. (TRG.)

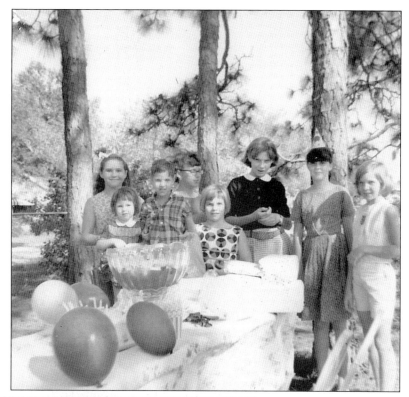

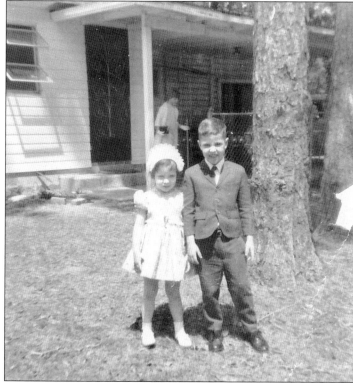

Teresa and Jim Rabon are ready for Easter Sunday services *c.* 1968. (TRG.)

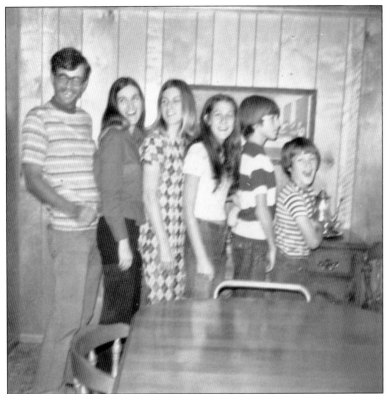

J. T. and Margaret Duncan and their six children lived at 1609 Arthur Avenue. An electrician, Duncan worked with Otis Freeman at Freeman Electric, which later became Lighted Signs by Freeman, owned and operated by Duncan. The brothers and sisters are, from left to right, Tommy, Cathy, Nancy, Debbie, Michael, and Steve c. 1970. (MAD.)

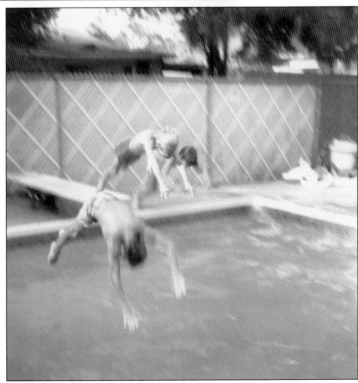

Mike (left) and Steve Duncan (right) and a friend dive into the pool in the Duncans' backyard. It was a favorite place for cousins and friends on a hot afternoon. (MAD.)

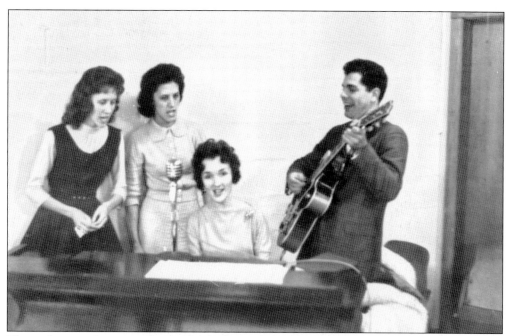

These photographs were taken at St. Andrews Assembly of God. From left to right are Lillian Barr, Joyce Barr, Rosella Ridings, and evangelist Richard Ronsisvalle with the guitar. (HRR.)

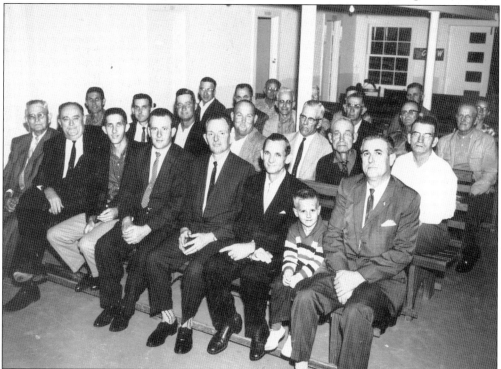

This men's fellowship meeting included, from left to right, (first row) unidentified, West Florida Assembly of God superintendent Rev. O. L. Thomas, Doug Barr, Pastor Howard Ridings, W. L. Miller, ? Dykes, H. Dean Ridings (the pastor's son) and unidentified. (HRR.)

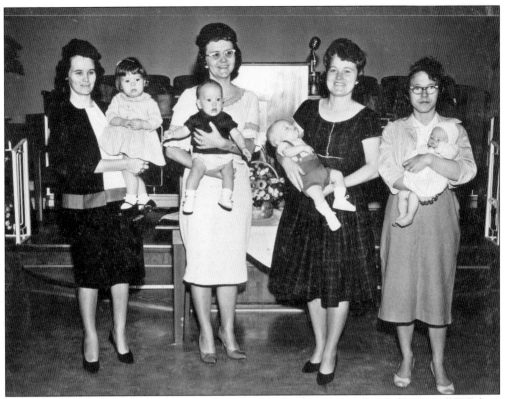

Peggy Kelly, second from left, is among these women bringing babies for dedication. (HRR.)

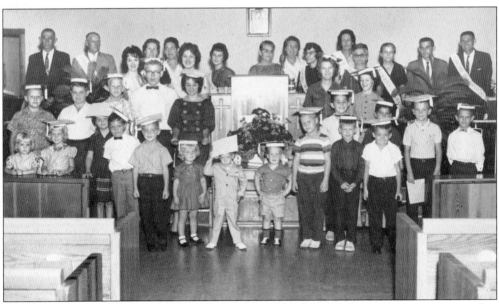

It is Sunday school graduation at St. Andrew's Assembly of God and time to move up to another class. (HRR.)

Seven

THE HILL

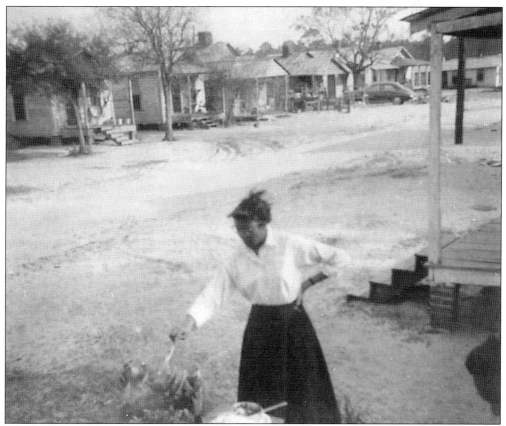

An early street scene in the Hill community shows a row of houses and a woman cooking outdoors, as was so often done. The neighborhood was settled on one of the highest points in St. Andrews and is recounted by Marlene Womack as "a notable settlement" where "the Longs, Covingtons, Williams, [Whitfields], and many other families settled, having come here in search of good jobs provided by the sawmill and turpentine industries." (RC.).

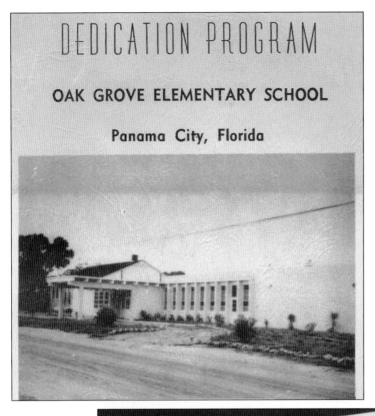

DEDICATION PROGRAM

OAK GROVE ELEMENTARY SCHOOL

Panama City, Florida

This is the new Oak Grove School, which opened at 1527 Lincoln Avenue in 1962. The Hill community started the first school for blacks in Bay County, St. Andrews Negro School, in 1910. The school operated three to four months annually and was housed in a variety of settings, including a local church in the community, until 1962. (RC.)

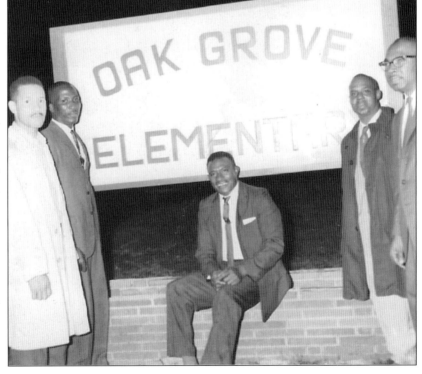

Walter Ford, Alphonso Williams, Jack Phillips, Walter Leverette, and Robert Cain are shown from left to right at Oak Grove Elementary School. (RC.)

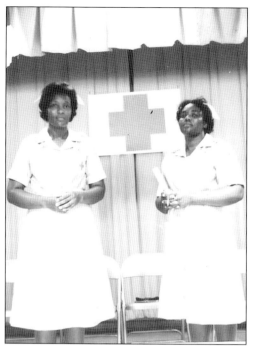
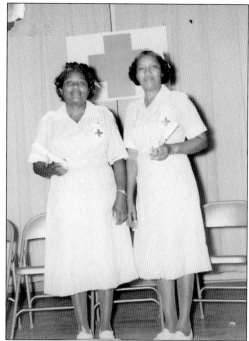

These Gray Ladies (Red Cross volunteers) are, from left to right, Alberta Phillips, Treather Deloach, Viola Cain, and Henrietta Long. (RC.)

Prof. Homer Jackson, lecturer, philosopher, poet, writer, and speaker, came to Bay County during World War II and settled on "The Hill." He and his wife, Helen, created a business program for black secondary students on their property. During his 40 years with the Bay County School District, he served as principal at several schools, including Oak Grove Elementary School on the Hill. The learning center at Patterson Elementary School is named in his honor. (RC.)

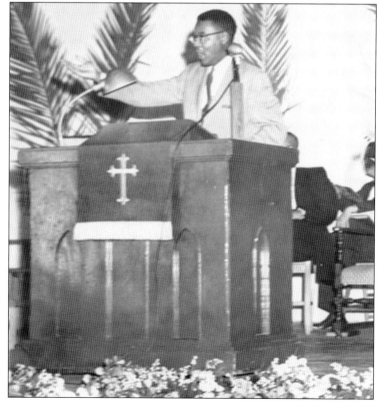

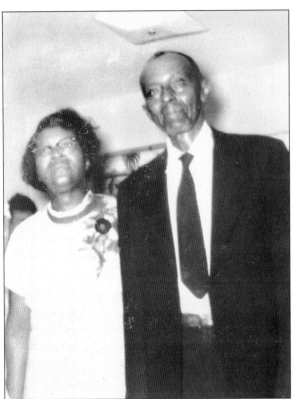

Claude Rhone and Marie Williams Rhone, in 1948, lived at 1503 Frankford Avenue in the community known as the Hill. (RC.)

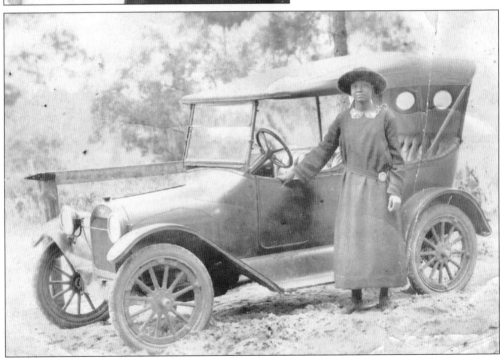

Mandy Lucas in the 1930s is shown standing by her car. Mandy was the wife of Henry Lucas, brother to Early Lucas. (JL.)

Rev. Early and Jessie Lucas moved to the Hill in the mid-1920s from Cordele, Georgia. They purchased land in the St. Andrews area (the Hill) and sold parcels to other settlers. Reverend Lucas founded the Jesus Only Tabernacle Church in 1948. Early and Jessie Lucas lived at 146 Fortune Avenue. (JL.)

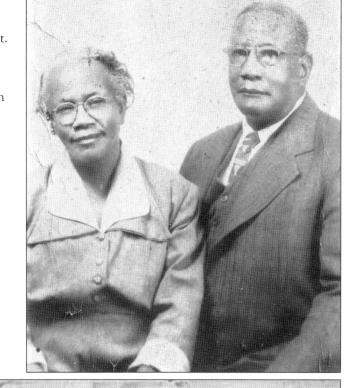

Taken in the late 1950s, this photograph shows members of the Jesus Only Tabernacle, founded by Rev. Early Lucas. Elders of the church seated in front from left to right are Mother Coley Blakely, Rev. Jessie Lucas, and evangelist Gertrude Lucas. (JL.)

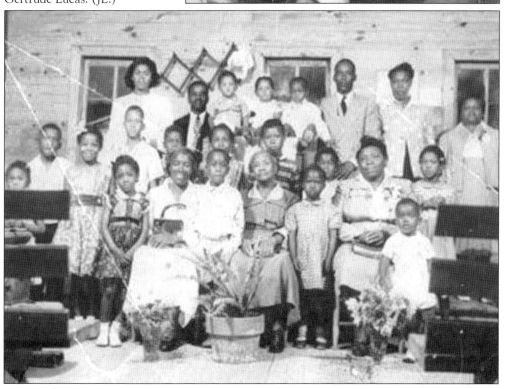

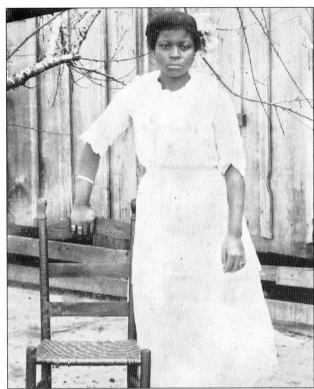

Priscilla Stephens, great-great-grandmother of Robert Cain, came here from Jackson County. In spite of blindness, Stephens was an accomplished homemaker and a leader in the community. (RC.)

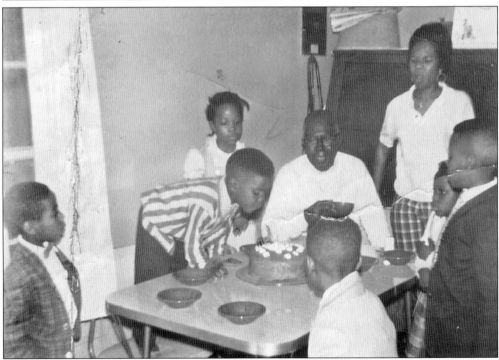

An unidentified youngster blows out the candles on his birthday cake in this photograph of a party group. (RC.)

Eight

DRUMMOND PARK

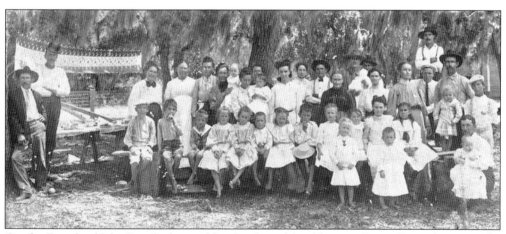

On the Fourth of July, Sam Surber and his family and neighbors on Pretty Bayou hung out the bunting, made tables of sawhorses and planks, and spread out the food. Notice there are no shoes on the children. (SF.)

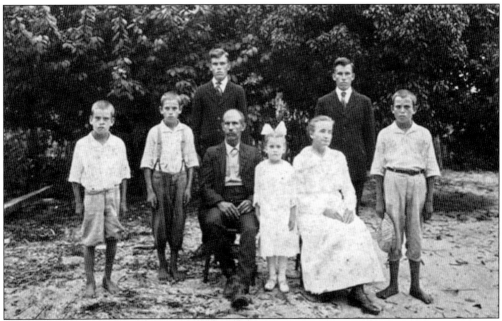

In this portrait of the Surbers, family members are, from left to right, Charles ("Turk"), Emmett, Cecil, Sam (seated), Elma, Neta (seated), Raymond, and Roy. Note Neta's button shoes. Boys at that time hardly ever wore shoes. (SF.)

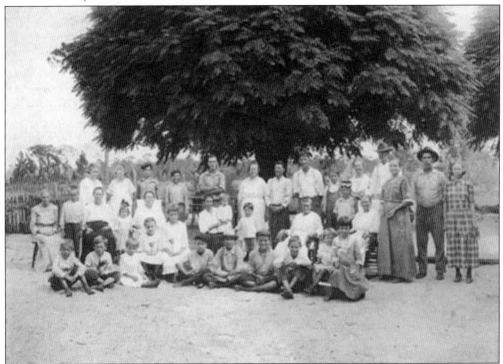

Another July Fourth picnic was held on Pretty Bayou, and friends and neighbors of the Surbers gathered under the big oak tree to spread out the food and celebrate the holiday. Sam and Neta Surber are standing far right. (SF.)

Roy (left) and Emmett Surber stand by the porch of their home on Pretty Bayou. Note that little boys of that day wore skirts until they were five or six years old, when they graduated to short pants. (SF.)

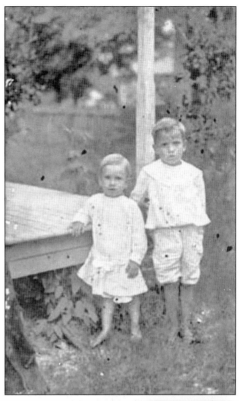

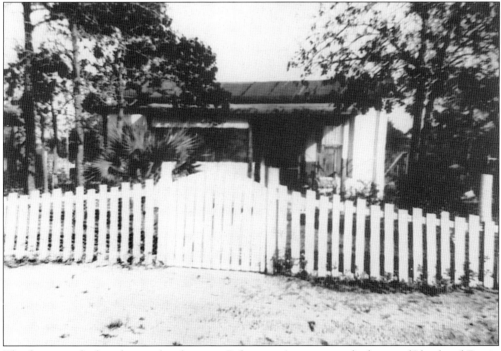

This house with the white picket fence on Baltimore Avenue was the home of Lloyd and Bertie Lee Nelson. (TSV.)

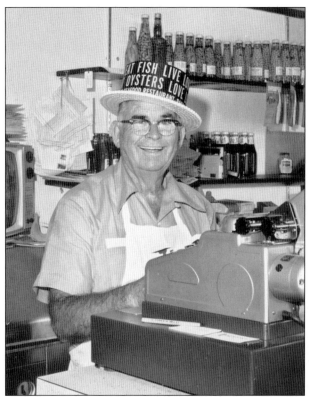

In 1971, Jesse R. Allen coined the slogan "Eat Fish Live Longer; Eat Oysters Love Longer at Allen's Seafood Restaurant." He printed fluorescent-green bumper stickers (note his hat) to advertise. Allen made all the sauces on the top shelf behind him in this photograph. He started cooking on party boats as a young man. (AO.)

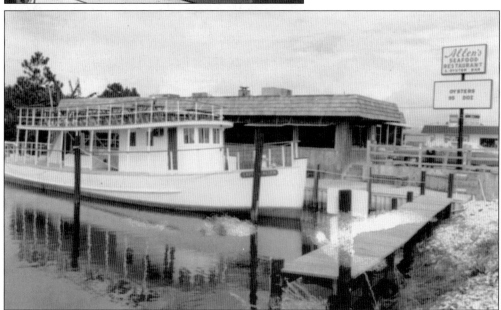

The boat *Capt. Allen*, docked alongside Allen's Seafood Restaurant, served as an oyster bar for overflow crowd waiting to be seated. Note the chairs on the top deck. The sign says "Oysters 95 [cents for a] doz[en]." You could get oysters on the half shell or by the bucket, shrimp, ice, live shrimp for bait, and tackle, and you could rent a boat and motor in the beginning, when Allen first opened for business. Later it became a full-service restaurant. (AO.)

Jesse Allen, center, is shown in Allen's Seafood Restaurant with all his workers. Jesse and his wife, Ruby, had three children—Derrell, Jessie May, and Mary Alice—and grandsons Ashley Olive and Aaron Allen. (AO.)

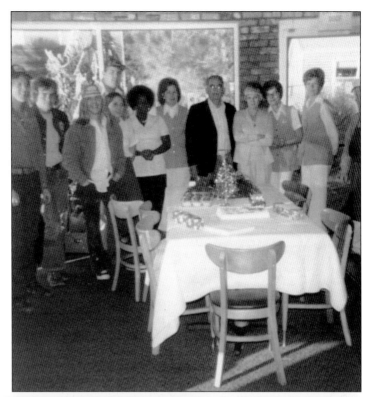

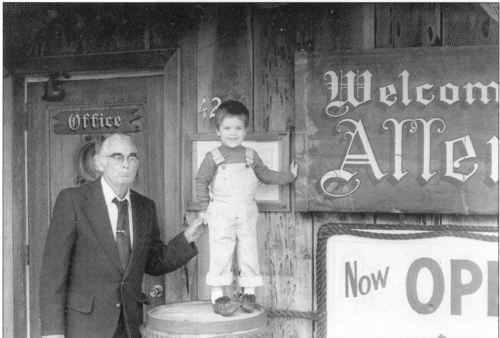

Jesse Allen stands in front of the restaurant with his grandson Aaron Allen c. 1978. Aaron is now CEO of Quantified Marketing, a restaurant management group. He is the son of Derrell Allen. (AO.)

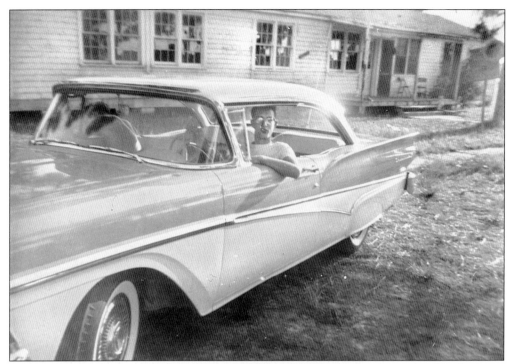

Wayne Lowe is sitting in the driver's seat of Tony McBride's new car at Drummond Park. A row of the houses that were built for Wainwright Shipyard workers is in the background. (TSV.)

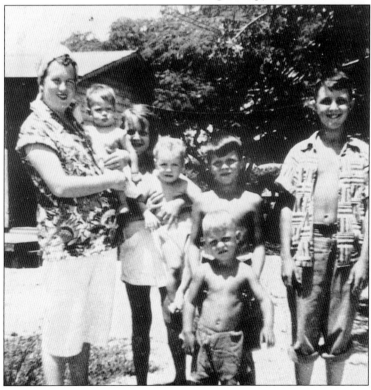

This group includes, from left to right, Mary Destifina, holding Susan; Marian Nelson, holding her sister Evelyn; brothers Philip (front) and Don; and Woodrow Wilson Jr. ("Tony"). (TSV.)

Irene Lowe, left, poses with Buck Nelson and Dan Stockwell, right, owner of a motel located at Baltimore Avenue and Highway 98. (TSV.)

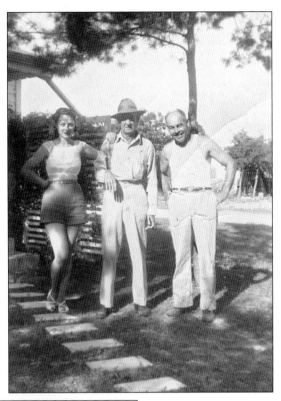

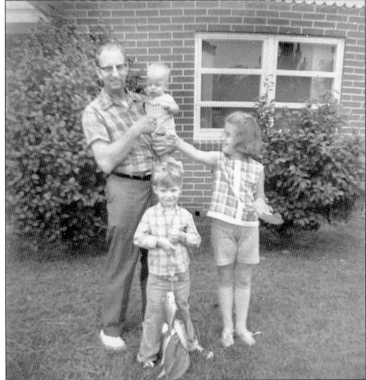

This family photograph shows, from left to right, Angus Scott holding Thomas; J. R. with fish; and Terry, at home on Lombardy Avenue. (TSV.)

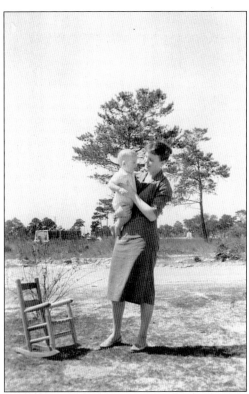

Marian McBride Scott holds her daughter, Terry, in 1962. Note Terry's little rocking chair. (TSV.)

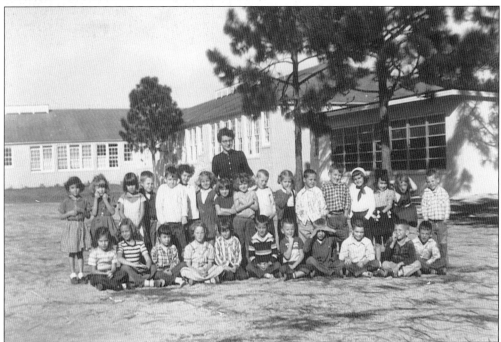

This class at Drummond Park School poses for a picture outside the building. No date or identifications were provided. The school was later named Lucille Moore Elementary School in honor of a longtime educator in Bay County. (TSV.)

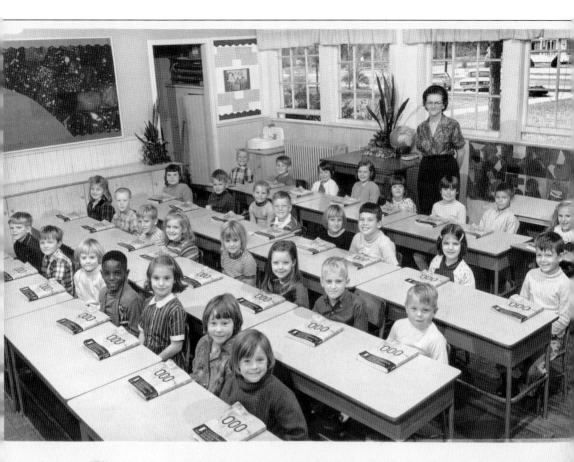

Marguerite Williamson

TEACHER   1ST GRADE

DRUMMOND PARK ELEMENTARY SCHOOL
PANAMA CITY, FLORIDA

Milton Acton

PRINCIPAL

1968 - 1969

Marguerite Williamson's first graders at Drummond Park Elementary School in 1968–1969 include, from left to right, (first row) Ray Hickman, three unidentified, Sherry Robinson, and two unidentified; (second row) Terry Scott, three unidentified, Janie Knutchek, unidentified, Greg Lewis, and unidentified; (third row) unidentified, David Merchant, Tim Kelly, unidentified, Beth Raynor, two unidentified, and Trey Shiftlett; (fourth row) seven unidentified and Tonya Burleson. Note the cloakroom door, the sink, and the radiator in the back and the nice windows with a view of cars. (TSV.)

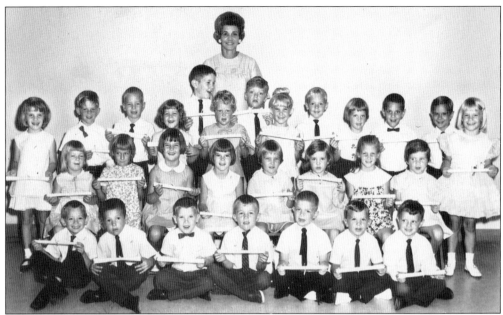

Mrs. Zediker, back row, center; is shown with her kindergarten class in 1967–1968. The only children identified are (second row) second from left, Beth Raynor; fifth from left Dana Smith; (third row) far left, Terry Scott; second from left, Ray Hickman; seventh from left, Kelly Roberts; eight from left, David Fretwell; and far right, Virginia Lowe. (TSV.)

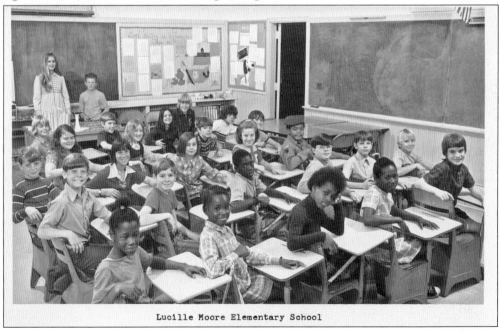

Kathy Ullman (Barr) is pictured with her fifth grade class at Lucille Moore Elementary School in 1972–1973. The school had previously been renamed to honor the longtime teacher/administrator. Included in this photo are Valerie Pinkerton, Sherry Robinson, Jimmy Nolan, David Sheffield, Lester Jenkins, Brian Morgan, Warren belt, Trey Gay, Bill Dozier, Robert Champion, Dottie Gray, Gary Elmore, and Terry Scott. (TSV.)

Katie Lee Nelson McBride is pictured on Baltimore Avenue. (TSV.)

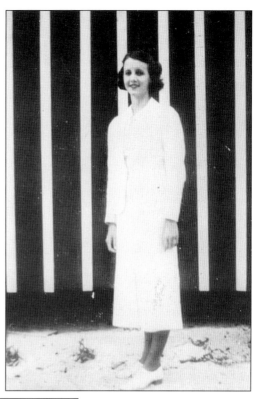

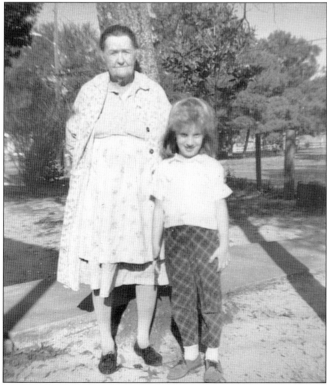

Kate Lee Nelson, left, is pictured with Terry Scott Vickmark c. 1970. (TSV.)

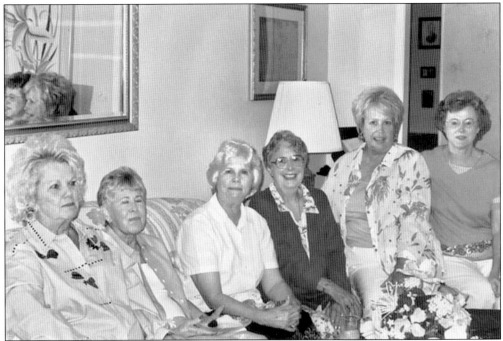

This reunion of friends who grew up together took place in October 2004. Pictured from left to right are Barbara Robinson, Jan Brittain Masseo, Ann Tew Cayns, Eve Taylor, Bette Surber Petitjean, and Patsy Roberts Higdon. (SF.)

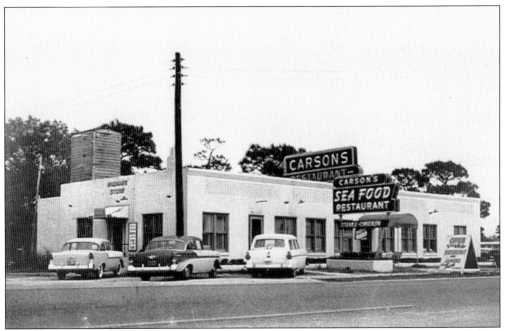

Carson's Restaurant at 3100 West Highway 98 in St. Andrews is shown in a 1957 postcard. Jimmy Mann was owner of the family restaurant, which featured seafood, steaks, and chicken. The package store is at left. (BCPL.)

Nine

OAKLAND TERRACE

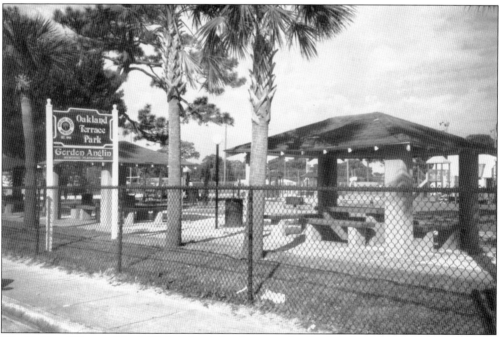

The Oakland Terrace Men's Club dedicated a plaque to the Gordon Anglin Memorial Playground at the Oakland Terrace Park on November 26, 2004. The inscription reads: "1918–2002. A loyal member of the Oakland Terrace Men's Club who devoted many years to see that our children have only the very best in this, 'His' Play Ground." Oakland Terrace Park has been a center for sports events and community meetings for many years. (BCPL.)

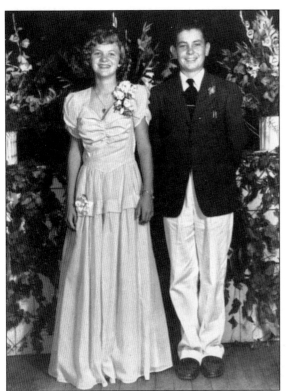

Patsy Cauley and Bill Newberry, students at Drummond Park School, were elected Queen and King of the May at a c. 1948 May Day Festival sponsored by Oakland Terrace Men's club for Oakland Terrace and Drummond Park Schools combined. (PCM.)

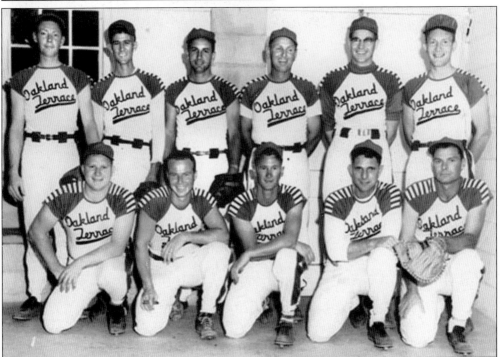

Pictured is the Oakland Terrace fast-pitch softball team in 1957. No identification was given. (BCPL.)

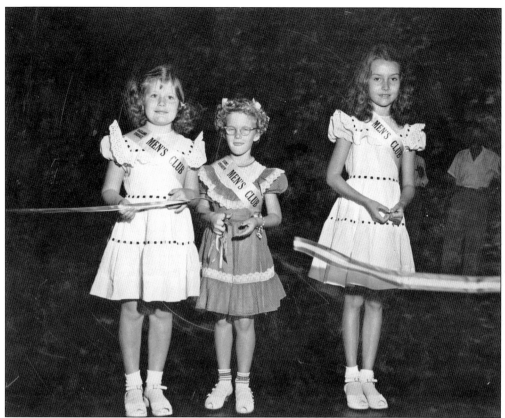

Participating in an Oakland Terrace Men's Club ribbon-cutting ceremony c. 1948 are, from left to right, Ann Lisenby, Karen Ann Davis, and Marie Lisenby. (BCPL.)

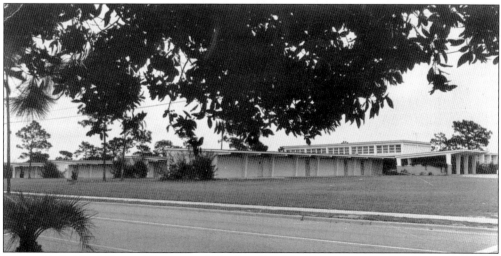

Pictured is Oakland Terrace Elementary School on Frankford Avenue on Twelfth Street. (OTES.)

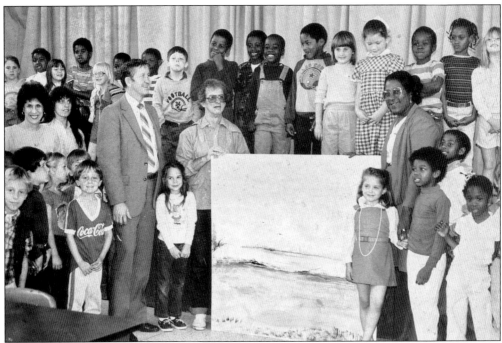

This photograph was made *c.* 1970 during an art presentation at Oakland Terrace Elementary School. Included are Kathy Lopez, Leonard Hall, unidentified presenter, Henrietta Swilley, and unidentified students from left to right. (OTES.)

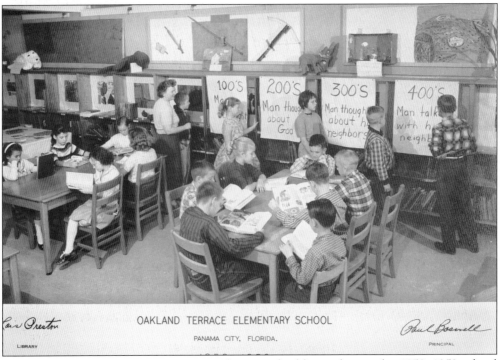

Librarian Lois Preston is instructing students in the library during the 1958–1959 school year. (OTES.)

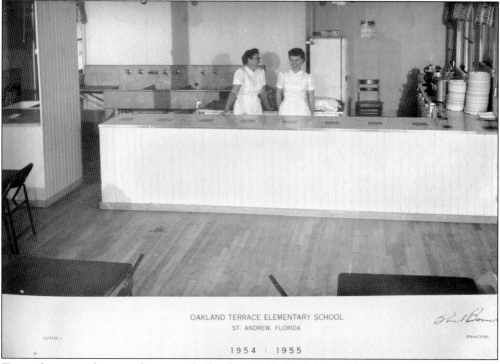

Two cafeteria workers are shown in the kitchen 1954–1955. (OTES.)

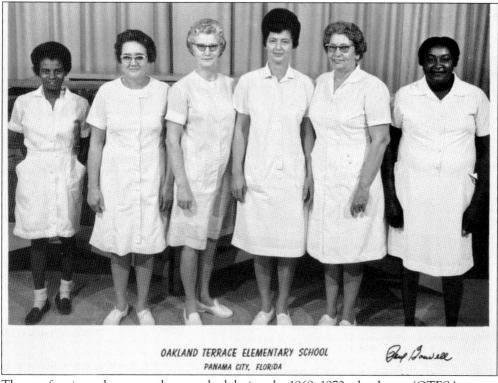

These cafeteria workers were photographed during the 1969–1970 school year. (OTES.)

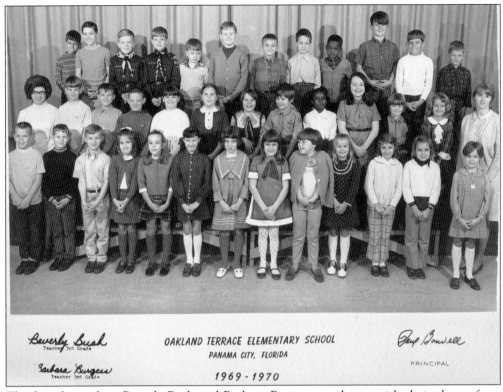

Third-grade teachers Beverly Bush and Barbara Burgess are shown with their classes from 1969–1970. (OTES.)

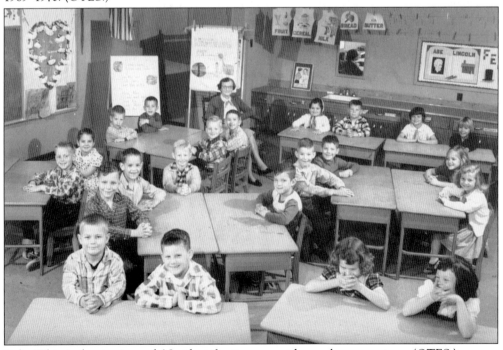

Ruby White's class is pictured. No identifications or grade number were given. (OTES.)

Ten

St. Andrews
Redevelopment and
Revitalization

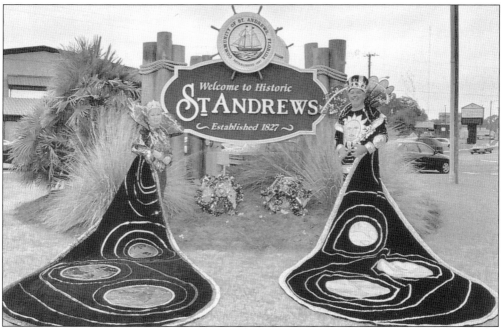

The St. Andrews community fell into decline in the 1970s. The City of Panama City established a Community Redevelopment Area in 1989 to help facilitate restoration of the community. The Krewe of St. Andrews drew attention to St. Andrews with the annual St. Andrews Mardi Gras Parade starting in 1997. Pictured at the Beck Avenue/Highway 98 St. Andrews sign are king and queen Bill and Terri Lillard in 2003. (SAWP.)

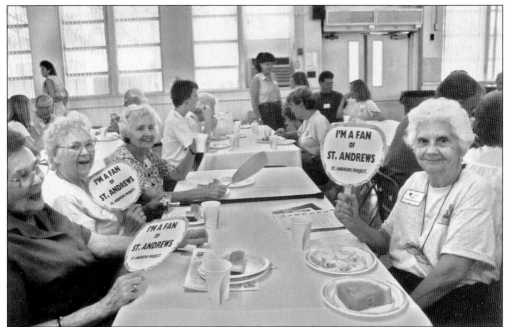

In 1995–1997, hundreds of citizens participated in a community visioning project that culminated in a document for guiding revitalization of the area and an established citizens group (St. Andrews Waterfront Partnership) to continue the effort. The St. Andrews "Fans" at this table are, from left to right, Rena Dell Windham, unidentified, Carlton Price, and Sara West. (SAWP.)

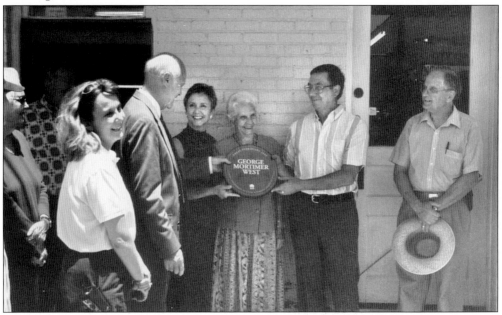

In 2001, Mayor Girard ("Gerry") Clemons presented a Florida Department of State "Great Floridian" plaque to the West family. George Mortimer West received the honor of "Great Floridian" for his contributions to the development of Panama City and the Bay County area in its early years. Pictured are Mayor Clemons, Margaret West Matheson, Sara West, Charles "Buddy" West, and Robert Hurst. (SAWP.)

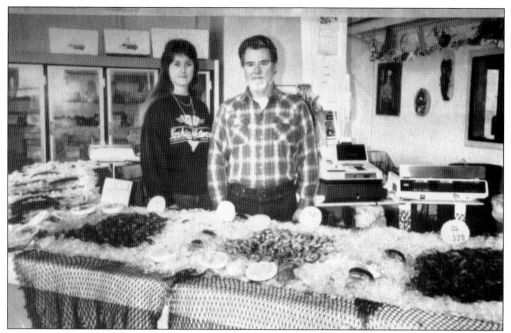

In the visioning process, the original St. Andrews neighborhoods were defined on a map, and this was the basis for the chapters of this book. Some families had influence in several neighborhoods of St. Andrews and Bay County, like the Gandy family, which operated the icehouse on Beck Avenue and a seafood market currently located on Highway 98. Pictured are Kenneth O. "Buddy" Gandy and his wife. (BCPL.)

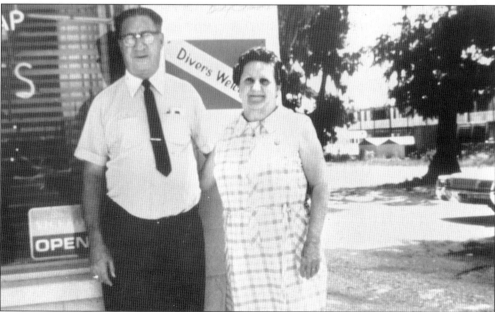

Pappy's was originally located in what is now the parking lot at Oaks by the Bay Park on West Tenth Street. Pictured are Charley and Kati Bierbaum, who moved from St. Louis and opened Pappy's in the 1960s. Since 1982, Christine Jamieson and her family have continued to run Pappy's German Restaurant, located in the next block at Tenth and Bayview. (CJ.)

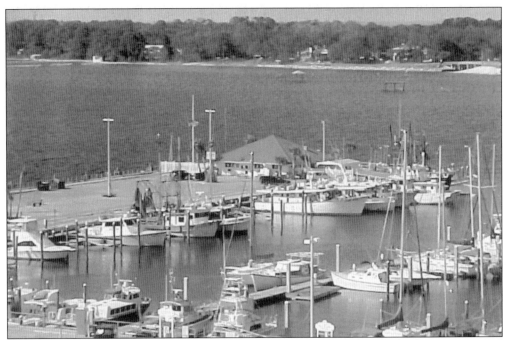

The renovated St. Andrews Marina reopened in 2002 and is bustling with charter, tour, and commercial activity. This view is from the Harbour Village condominium, constructed on the former Ramada Inn and Harbour House Restaurant site. (SAWP.)

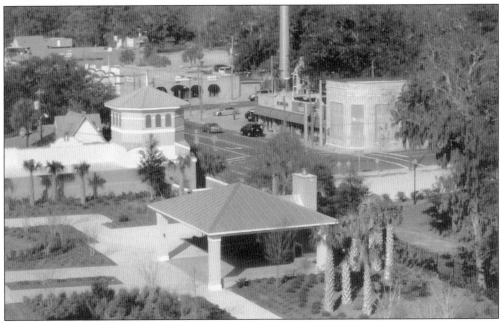

Another beautiful view from Harbour Village shows the rooftop garden of the complex and Oaks by the Bay Park to the right. The historic bank on the right corner is shown under renovation by Coastal Community Bank, with restored shops and St. Andrews Coffeehouse next to it. On the left side is the peaked roof of what was Le Shack Restaurant for many years, currently the Granite Café. The building was a Pure Oil gas station constructed in the 1940s. (SAWP.)

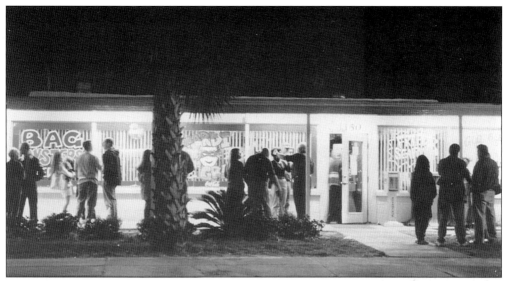

St. Andrews is coming to life again. This picture shows patrons waiting to get into Hunt's, a popular seafood restaurant since the 1960s. (SAWP.)

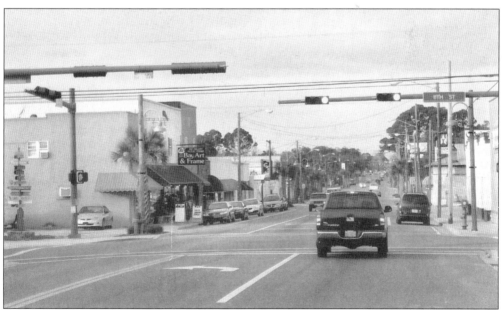

Beck Avenue is shown in 2007. On the left is longtime St. Andrews business Bay Art and Frame, where many artists have painted the sights of St. Andrews over the years. Renowned watercolor artist Dean Mitchell had his first one-man show here in the late 1970s. (SAWP.)

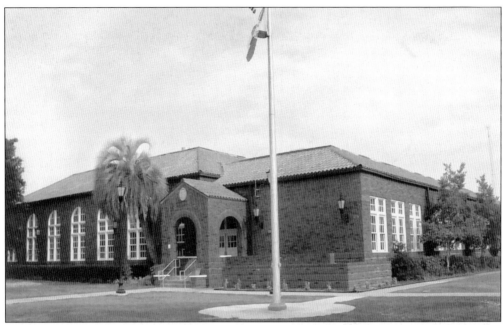

A restoration project between 1999 and 2002 preserved the 1926 St. Andrews School building, and it was listed on the National Register of Historic Places. (SAWP.)

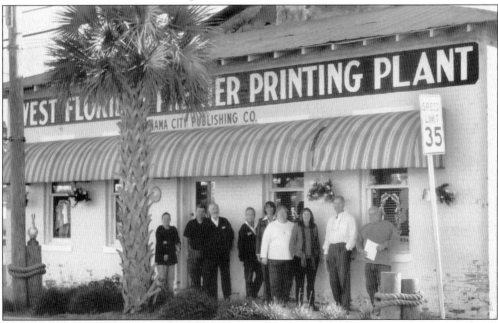

The Panama City Publishing Company building, constructed in 1920 by George M. West, contains the original printing presses and office furnishings. The city received a grant from the Department of State Bureau of Historic Preservation in 2006 for restoration of the building. Pictured from left to right are 2007 St. Andrews Waterfront Partnership representatives: Juli Hudson, Craig Thurmond (president), Al Kidd, Lena Powell, Alisa James (history committee chair), Dianne Eaton, Lorne Brooks Brumm (treasurer), Panama City commissioner John E. Pilcher III, and Bill Bruhmuller (vice president). (SAWP.)

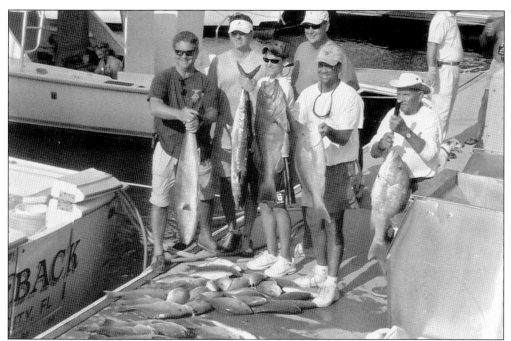

The fishing is still fine in St. Andrews. (SAWP.)

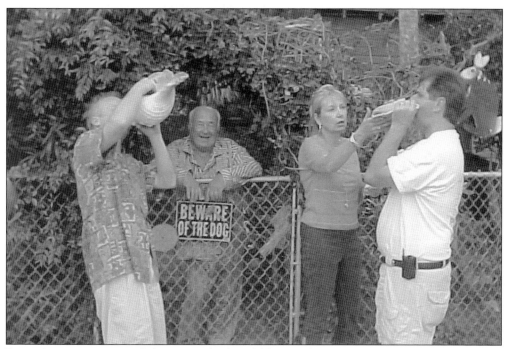

Every day at sunset, conch horns can be heard blowing from various corners of St. Andrews. Bill Tant is the "resident conch" in charge of sales and instruction. Here West End residents John Flowers (left) and Bill Sheffield (right) receive instructions from Tant (at gate) and Jan Sheffield. (SAWP.)

Across America, People are Discovering Something Wonderful. Their Heritage.

Arcadia Publishing is the leading local history publisher in the United States. With more than 3,000 titles in print and hundreds of new titles released every year, Arcadia has extensive specialized experience chronicling the history of communities and celebrating America's hidden stories, bringing to life the people, places, and events from the past. To discover the history of other communities across the nation, please visit:

www.arcadiapublishing.com

Customized search tools allow you to find regional history books about the town where you grew up, the cities where your friends and family live, the town where your parents met, or even that retirement spot you've been dreaming about.

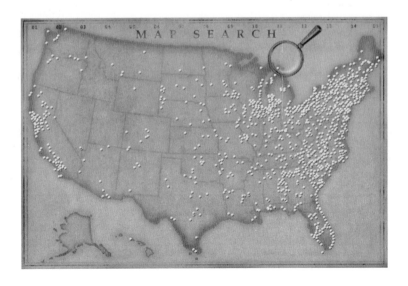